ABSTRACT

United States military involvement in foreign humanitarian assistance operations should meet strategic parameters that support U.S. national security interests. Foreign humanitarian assistance demonstrates U.S. goodwill and support for national governments in times of need, and also offers the United States an opportunity to demonstrate U.S. values abroad, support human rights, and enhance regional security. If not orchestrated in the context of pursuing national security interests, U.S. military involvement in foreign humanitarian assistance operations can largely be ineffectual opportunities that consume precious and ever scarcer resources, overextend the military, and often put Americans in danger. U.S. military foreign humanitarian assistance operations, a powerful and effective non-kinetic element of national power, should be grounded in U.S. strategic purpose and used judiciously to mitigate human suffering in the event of natural or man-made disasters. This paper will review relevant terms and definitions as well as discuss the theories of Realism and Idealism in international relations. Analysis of current U.S. strategic guidance establishes the contemporary context of U.S. military involvement in foreign humanitarian assistance operations. Two historical case studies will be presented: the Berlin Airlift (1948-1949) and Somalia (1992-1994). The analysis of these case studies will illustrate how well the operations supported U.S. national security interests. The analysis will also provide a basis for recommendations to define parameters for U.S. policymakers that link U.S. military involvement in foreign humanitarian assistance operations to U.S. national security interests.

TABLE OF CONTENTS

This page intentionally blank

INTRODUCTION

Use of military forces for humanitarian purposes is a long-established tradition in all corners of the world. In the public mind, there is an association between disaster relief and military involvement; indeed, there is often an expectation that military units will assist the civilian population in the immediate aftermath of wars and large-scale emergencies.[1]

Foreign humanitarian assistance demonstrates U.S. goodwill and support for national governments in times of need, and also offers the United States an opportunity to highlight the advantages of democracy and support human rights and regional security.[2] Because the U.S. military's role in foreign humanitarian assistance operations has been so prominent since the end of the Cold War, many people throughout the world have come to expect intervention and relief from the United States in the wake of disaster. The considerable capabilities of the U.S. military to alleviate suffering in times of hardship certainly provide opportunities to influence the way people perceive the United States. However, if not connected to larger national security interests, military support for foreign humanitarian assistance operations can serve to waste scarce resources, divert high demand and low density assets, and lower overall readiness of U.S. military forces.

In the face of almost certain budget cuts over the next decade, U.S. military forces will struggle to maintain a balanced force capable of conducting a wide variety of missions. Resource constraints will force the military to be far more focused on high priority national security goals to avoid being what President Obama describes in the

---

[1] Frederick C. Cuny, International Disaster Relief Specialist, "Use of the Military in Humanitarian Relief," speech given at Niinsalo, Finland Military Academy, November, 1989, "Frontline, PBS Online. http://www.pbs.org/wgbh/pages/frontline/shows/cuny/laptop/humanrelief html (accessed September 9, 2012), 1. Mr. Cuny helped found the International Crisis Group and was active in many humanitarian projects around the world from 1969 until his forced disapearance in Chechnya in 1995.

[2] Chairman of the Joint Chiefs of Staff, *2010 Joint Professional Military Education (JPME) Special Areas of Emphasis*, May 17, 2010 (Washington DC: Department of Defense, 17 May 2010).

U.S. National Security Strategy as "overstretched:"

> But when we overuse our military might, or fail to invest in or deploy complementary tools, or act without partners, then our military is overstretched, Americans bear a greater burden, and our leadership around the world is too narrowly identified with military force.[3]

In the 2013 State of the Union Address, while describing his vision to meet the threat posed by Al Qaeda affiliates and extremist groups, President Obama reinforced his desire to minimize future large-scale military operations, "we don't need to send tens of thousands of our sons and daughters abroad or occupy other nations."[4]

To maintain a proper balance U.S. military involvement in foreign humanitarian assistance operations should meet strategic parameters that support U.S. national security interests. U.S. military involvement in foreign humanitarian assistance, often described as part of national "soft power," can provide effective support to the diplomatic element of national power.[5] However, the use of the U.S. military to support diplomacy should be grounded in U.S. strategic purpose, and be used deliberately and judiciously to support U.S. national security interests. U.S. leaders and policymakers need to understand within what strategic parameters the U.S. military can be used to support foreign humanitarian assistance operations.

This paper will begin with a review of selected terms to interpret and establish respective definitions and clarify the vernacular used in the context of this study. The paper will analyze doctrinal definitions, determine their adequacy and suggest changes if applicable. Next, a review of international relations theories will be used to develop an understanding of the foundation of U.S. national security strategy and the approach U.S.

---

[3] U.S. President. *National Security Strategy.* Washington DC: Government Printing Office, May 2010, 18.
[4] U.S. President. *2013 State of the Union Address,* February 12, 2013.
[5] Joseph Nye, Jr., *Soft Power, The Means to Success in World Politics* (New York: PublicAffairs, 2004), IX.

leaders may use to determine how and when to use the military to support foreign humanitarian assistance operations.

A review of strategic guidance will inform analysis and develop an understanding of contemporary strategic perspectives and guidance provided by U.S. national leaders and policymakers. The National Security Strategy (NSS), Presidential Policy Directives (PPD), National Defense Strategy (NDS), Quadrennial Defense Review (QDR), National Military Strategy (NMS), Department of State Quadrennial Diplomacy and Development Review (QDDR), and U.S. Department of Defense doctrine, policy and guidance will be analyzed to establish how contemporary U.S. leaders and policymakers characterize foreign humanitarian assistance.

Two historical case studies of U.S. military supported foreign humanitarian assistance operations will be presented: the Berlin Airlift (1948-1949) and Somalia (1992-1994). The Berlin Airlift will provide an illustration of using a realist political approach to achieve U.S. national security interests using military power to support foreign humanitarian assistance operations. Conversely, a review of U.S. military intervention in Somalia fifty-five years later, dampened by political challenges, will illustrate an idealist political approach where military activities in support of foreign humanitarian assistance operations did not fully support U.S. national security interests. Analysis of the case studies will provide a historical perspective to help establish a basis for recommendations to define parameters for U.S. leaders and policymakers to consider when linking U.S. military involvement in foreign humanitarian assistance operations to U.S. national security interests.

This page intentionally blank

CHAPTER 1

HUMANITARIAN ASSISTANCE AND NATIONAL INTERESTS

Definitions

For clarity, it is important to establish and understand definitions of selected terms used in the context of this study: *Humanitarian Assistance, Foreign Humanitarian Assistance, Foreign Assistance, Foreign Disaster Relief, National Interests,* and *Levels of Intensity for National Interests.* These terms, integral to this study, are often used inconsistently by U.S. leaders, policymakers, and military professionals. Consequently, their definitions are not standardized across the whole of government, and can often imply different things to different people depending on the context in which the words are used. Moreover, words can be used in a certain context to justify certain actions, while being used differently by another department or agency in a different situation leading to U.S. government interagency confusion which often contributes to leaders and agencies talking past one another.

Humanitarian Assistance

The U.S. Department of Defense definition:

> Programs conducted to relieve or reduce the results of natural or manmade disasters or other endemic conditions such as human pain, disease, hunger, or privation that might present a serious threat to life or that can result in great damage to or loss of property. Humanitarian assistance provided by U.S. forces is limited in scope and duration. The assistance provided is designed to supplement or complement the efforts of the host nation civil authorities or agencies that may have the primary responsibility for providing humanitarian assistance.[1]

The U.S. Department of State defines humanitarian assistance in these terms:

---

[1] U.S. Joint Chiefs of Staff, *Civil-Military Operations, Joint Publication 3-57* (Washington DC: Joint Chiefs of Staff, 8 July 2008), GL-9.

To save lives, alleviate suffering, and minimize the economic costs of conflict, disasters and displacement. Humanitarian assistance is provided on the basis of need according to principles of universality, impartiality and human dignity. It is often organized by sectors, but requires an integrated, coordinated and/or multi-sectoral approach to be most effective. Emergency operations will foster the transition from relief, through recovery, to development, but they cannot and will not replace the development investments necessary to reduce chronic poverty or establish just social services.[2]

Similar in content, both definitions share a moral premise to save lives or relieve, reduce or alleviate human suffering. Of note, in the first definition, the Department of Defense highlights that humanitarian assistance is "limited in scope and duration" and is "designed to supplement or complement the efforts of the host nation civil authorities or agencies." This codifies the Department of Defense's understanding that U.S. military support for humanitarian assistance operations will be short-term and provided in a supplemental role.

On the other hand, the Department of State definition for Humanitarian Assistance is broader in terms of describing a whole of government design; the definition describes an "integrated, coordinated and/or multi-sectoral approach" as a requirement to be effective. The definition does not describe the U.S. military's role nor does it provide an expected timeline for military involvement in humanitarian assistance operations. The Department of State definition refers to several transitions, from "relief, through recovery, to development," implying that humanitarian assistance is a longer term effort than what is described by the Department of Defense. The definition also indicates that humanitarian assistance should "minimize the economic costs of conflicts, disasters and displacement," although the definition fails to specify the type of costs in

_____

[2] U.S. Department of State, *Standardized Program Structure and Definitions* (April 8, 2010): 85, http://www.state.gov/f/c24132 htm (accessed November 20, 2012).

terms of U.S. Department of State costs, U.S. military costs, host nation costs, or otherwise.

Foreign Humanitarian Assistance

The U.S. Department of Defense defines *Foreign Humanitarian Assistance* as "Department of Defense activities, normally in support of the United States Agency for International Development (USAID) or Department of State, conducted outside the United States, its territories, and possessions to relieve or reduce human suffering, disease, hunger, or privation."[3] The definition highlights the premise that the U.S. military, under most circumstances, will not be designated the lead U.S. agency in foreign humanitarian assistance operations. The Department of Defense distinguishes between "humanitarian assistance" and "foreign humanitarian assistance" to differentiate humanitarian assistance operations conducted within the United States from foreign humanitarian assistance operations conducted outside the United States. Under extreme disaster conditions, the U.S. military may provide Defense Support of Civil Authorities (DSCA) while supporting humanitarian assistance operations to aid U.S. citizens residing in the United States.

Foreign Assistance

The Department of Defense describes *Foreign Assistance* as "assistance to foreign nations ranging from the sale of military equipment to donations of food and medical supplies to aid survivors of natural and manmade disasters. U.S. foreign assistance takes three forms: development assistance, humanitarian assistance, and security assistance."[4]

---

[3] U.S. Joint Chiefs of Staff, *Foreign Humanitarian Assistance, Joint Publication 3-29* (Washington DC: Joint Chiefs of Staff, 17 March 2009), GL-8.
[4] U.S. Joint Chiefs of Staff, *Foreign Humanitarian Assistance, Joint Publication 3-29* (Washington DC: Joint Chiefs of Staff, 17 March 2009), GL-7.

This definition highlights that foreign humanitarian assistance is only one of three types of U.S. foreign assistance, although the definition can be confusing as it specifically refers to "aid survivors of natural and man-made disasters." This wording is more in line with "foreign disaster relief," although it is not specifically listed in the definition as one of the three forms of U.S. foreign assistance. This observation is subtle but it is important to understand, that for the purpose of this study, foreign disaster relief will be considered a subset of foreign humanitarian assistance and the two terms will not be identified separately; all references to foreign humanitarian assistance will include foreign disaster relief considerations as both operations share similarities from a U.S. military-support perspective.

Foreign Disaster Relief

The Department of Defense defines *Foreign Disaster Relief*:

> Military operations that support prompt aid that can be used to alleviate the suffering of foreign disaster victims. Normally it includes humanitarian services and transportation; the provision of food, clothing, medicine, beds, and bedding; temporary shelter and housing; the furnishing of medical materiel and medical and technical personnel; and making repairs to essential services.[5]

Historical analysis indicates that regardless of a nation's or population's strategic value, the United States leans favorably to offering support in some capacity for foreign disaster relief efforts, often leading with military logistical capabilities to help save lives, alleviate immediate suffering and maintain the basic human dignity of foreign disaster victims.

National Interests

Closely examining how the term *national interest* is defined and largely interpreted by scholars and policymakers is essential to this study. So what exactly are

---

[5] U.S. Joint Chiefs of Staff, *Foreign Humanitarian Assistance, Joint Publication 3-29* (Washington DC: Joint Chiefs of Staff, 17 March 2009), GL-8.

national interests? A review of contemporary literature suggests the term is ambiguous, as most scholars write their own definition of national interests rather than accept a common reference. Literature further suggests that most scholars describe what they believe national interests are, but few articulate how national interests are defined.[6]

The Department of Defense defines *national security interests* as "the foundation for the development of valid national objectives that define U.S. goals or purposes." National security interests are described as "preserving U.S. political...institutions; fostering economic well-being; and bolstering international order."[7] This definition helps establish that national interests are the foundation for developing national objectives that further help define goals and purposes in relation to the stated national security interests. National interests are often articulated and updated by the President in the National Security Strategy (NSS) and policy directives.

National interests are generally not threatened at the same time, although it is important to realize that U.S. national interests are so extensive that the U.S. Government cannot engage to protect every one of them. Dr. David Tucker articulates that the United States is a global power with global interests, "it is not enough to know that its interests are at stake in some problem or conflict, for every problem or conflict will impinge somehow on its interests."[8] Related to foreign humanitarian assistance, interests alone cannot be the determining factor to act; the interests must include contributions to bolstering international order.

[6] Paul B. Eberhart, *Grand Strategy of the United States: A Study of the Process* (Norfolk, VA: Joint Forces Staff College, 2009), 29.

[7] U.S. Joint Chiefs of Staff, Department of Defense Dictionary of Military and Associated Terms, Joint Publication 1-02 (Washington DC: Joint Chiefs of Staff, 12 April 2001), 287.

[8] Ambassador Robert B. Oakley and David Tucker, edited by Earl Tilford, Jr., *Two Perspectives on Interventions and Humanitarian Operations* (Carlisle Barracks: Army War College, 1997), 19.

Similar to the Department of Defense definition, Donald Nuechterlein, in *America Overcommitted: United States National Interests in the 1980's*, describes national interests as "the perceived needs and desires of a sovereign state in relation to other sovereign states that constitute its external environment."[9] Helpful to guiding national policymakers, Nuechterlein developed a conceptual framework that identifies four basic enduring national interests. Listed in priority order the interests are: 1) providing for defense of the homeland; 2) supporting the economic well-being of the nation; 3) building favorable world order; and 4) promoting the nation's value system abroad.[10] Nuechterlein's fourth enduring national interest regarding promoting U.S. values differentiates his definition from the Department of Defense definition. Other scholars, including Harry Yarger and Robert Art, offer very similar definitions of national interests in their writings.[11]

For this study Nuechterlein's definition and conceptual structure of national interests is preferred as his structure more closely resembles the framework of national interests identified in the most recent U.S. National Security Strategy. National interests will serve as the foundation for a working model that will be defined later in this study to identify parameters for U.S. policymakers to link U.S. military involvement in foreign humanitarian assistance operations to U.S. national security interests.

Levels of Intensity of National Interests

Beyond identifying specific national interests, Yarger offers reasons why it is important to assign a level of intensity to the interests once an interest is identified. A

---

[9] Harry Yarger, Strategy and the National Security Professional: Strategic Thinking and Strategy Formulation in the 21st Century (Westport: Praeger Security International, 2008), 118.

[10] Donald Nuechterlein, *Defiant Superpower: The New American Hegemony* (Washington DC: Potomac Books Inc., 2005), 58-60.

[11] Paul B. Eberhart, *Grand Strategy of the United States: A Study of the Process* (Norfolk, VA: Joint Forces Staff College, 2009), 32.

level of intensity suggests the relative importance and sense of urgency among competing interests, although it is important to be aware that a lower level of intensity does not imply the interest should be ignored. The level of intensity also assigns a weight of effort and risk acceptance implication to the interest. When assessing and assigning a level of intensity, Yarger cautions that the decision to act on a national interest does not come from the assignment of intensity itself, but rather the decision to act flows from the strategy formulation process.[12] Yarger identifies and defines four levels of intensity for national interests:

> SURVIVAL—if unfulfilled, will result in immediate massive destruction of one or more major aspects of the core national objectives.
> VITAL—if unfulfilled, will have immediate consequence for core national interests.
> IMPORTANT—if unfulfilled, will result in damage that will eventually affect core national interests.
> PERIPHERAL—if unfulfilled, will result in damage that is unlikely to affect core national interests.[13]

Nuechterlein adds a degree of precision and clarity to Yarger's levels of intensity:

> SURVIVAL (critical)—interests are rare and are relatively easy to identify. A survival interest is at stake when there is an imminent, credible threat of massive destruction to the homeland, physical existence of a country is in jeopardy due to attack or threat of attack.
> VITAL (dangerous)—interest differs from a survival one principally in the amount of time a country has to decide how it will respond to an external threat where serious harm to the nation would result unless strong measures, including the use of force, are employed to protect the interest.
> MAJOR (serious)—interest is one that a country considers to be important not crucial to its well-being. Major interests involve issues and trends, whether they are economic, political, or ideological, that can be negotiated with an adversary. Such issues may cause serious concern and even harm to U.S. interests abroad, but policymakers usually come to the conclusion that negotiation and compromise, rather than confrontation, are desirable—even though the result may be painful.

---

[12] Harry Yarger, Strategy and the National Security Professional: Strategic Thinking and Strategy Formulation in the 21st Century (Westport: Praeger Security Internaional, 2008), 122.
[13] Ibid.

PERIPHERAL (bothersome)—interest is one that does not seriously affect the well-being of the United States as a whole, even though it may be detrimental to the private interests of Americans conducting business abroad these are situations where some national interest is involved but where the country as a whole is not particularly affected by any given outcome or the impact is negligible.[14]

Robert Art, in *A Grand Strategy for America,* provides comprehensive definitions for three suggested levels of intensity, including a descriptive role for the potential use of military power:[15]

> VITAL—one that is essential and, if not achieved, will bring cost that are catastrophic or nearly so. Security is the one vital interest of a state; it means protection of the state's homeland from attack, invasion, conquest, and destruction. American military power can directly advance vital interests.
> HIGHLY IMPORTANT—on that, if achieved, brings great benefits to a state and, if denied, carries costs that are severe but not catastrophic. American military power can directly advance highly important interest.
> IMPORTANT—one that increases a nation's economic well-being and perhaps its security, and that contributes more generally to making the international environment more congenial to its interests, but whose potential value or loss is moderate, not great. American military power can only indirectly advance important interest.[16]

As presented, one sees that contemporary scholars offer similar descriptions, albeit with minor nuances, to categorize levels of intensity for national interests. This author believes the categories and descriptions were primarily intended to be used for kinetic military power. However, the categories and descriptions can also have a direct bearing on non-kinetic military power used to support foreign humanitarian assistance operations. Awareness of the varying categories and descriptions provides an appreciation for the level of thought scholars have attributed to this component and will

---

[14] Donald Nuechterlein, America Recommitted: A Superpower Assesses Its Role in a Turbulent World – Second Edition (Lexington, KY: University of Lexington Press, 2001), 17-20.

[15] Paul B. Eberhart, *Grand Strategy of the United States: A Study of the Process* (Norfolk, VA: Joint Forces Staff College, 2009), 36.

[16] Robert Art, *A Grand Strategy for America* (Ithaca, NY: Cornell University Press, 2003), 45-46.

prove useful later in this study as a framework is developed to suggest that U.S. military involvement in foreign humanitarian assistance operations should meet strategic parameters, related to objectives and goals in support of U.S. national security interests. A discussion of specific U.S. national interests and associated levels of intensity will follow later in this study when the current U.S. National Security Strategy and other national-level strategies and policies are analyzed.

This study has established definitions of select terms relating to foreign humanitarian assistance. To further an examination of national interests a description and brief analysis of international relations theory will help explain approaches used by U.S. national leaders and policymakers while making decisions to use the military to support foreign humanitarian assistance operations.

Realism versus Idealism

National leaders use their understanding of the world as the basis for decision-making. How national leaders perceive the United States' role in the world can be viewed through the lenses of various international relations theories. Over time, scholars have presented several international relations theories to help explain geopolitical relationships and subsequent agreements or disagreements among nation-states, organizations and non-state actors. The two most prevalent international relations theories are Realism and Idealism (identified by some scholars as Constructivism),[17] albeit both theories offer several variations. Realism and Idealism theories establish theoretical parameters for all other international relations theories. For the purpose of this study, an analysis of the fundamental differences between Realism and Idealism

---

[17] Stephen M. Walt, "International Relations: One World, Many Theories." *Foreign Policy*, 110, Spring, 1998, 29-35.

theories is warranted to help understand how national leaders are influenced. The decision to use the U.S. military to support foreign humanitarian assistance operations often lies politically in the middle position of Realism and Idealism theories.

The basic tenet of Realism is that all sovereign nations should act in their own self-interest to pursue or maintain power and security. Realism instills a pragmatic appreciation of the role of power to resolve national issues, and warns that states will suffer over time if they overreach and pursue objectives unrelated to national interests. The Realist believes a state's actions should be determined by the measures that accrue the most power to the nation. The Realist evaluates actions in terms of clearly achievable outcomes that result in gaining regional influence, advancing the security of the state, or ensuring an economic advantage.

Idealism theory in essence suggests that a state should make its internal political philosophy the goal of its foreign policy. International politics is shaped less by power than by persuasive ideas, collective values, and cultural and social identities. Idealists visualize the world as it might or should be and suggest a state's foreign policy should be guided by moral principles. Stephen Walt describes Idealism in these terms:

> Although power is not irrelevant, [idealism/] constructivism emphasizes
> how ideas and identities are created, how they evolve, and how they shape
> the way states understand and respond to their situation. Therefore, it
> matters whether Europeans define themselves primarily in national or
> continental terms; whether Germany and Japan redefine their pasts in
> ways that encourage their adopting more active international roles; and
> whether the United States embraces or rejects its identity as "global
> policeman."[18]

Idealists suggest that the capability of a state to assist also creates a duty to assist. Madeleine Albright, the U.S. Ambassador to the United Nations, promoted the

---

[18] Stephen M. Walt, "International Relations: One World, Many Theories." *Foreign Policy*, 110, Spring, 1998, 29-35.

idealist viewpoint at the end of the Cold War, "I believe that when the United States can make a difference, that we have a moral imperative to make a difference."[19]

In summary, Realism and Idealism theories help explain how national leaders perceive the United States' role in the world and the approach they may consider to determine how and when to use the U.S. military to support foreign humanitarian assistance operations. Realists tend to believe the United States should use power for concrete results that benefit the nation and bolster international order. Idealists believe that morals, principles, and values are prioritized over concrete realities like national interests. The United States' approach to foreign relations often lies somewhere in the middle of the two theories and vacillates between the two approaches due to each Presidential administration's view of the world. The environment of the time suggests this still may be the case.

In *Humanitarian Intervention and Just War*, Mona Fixdal and Dan Smith describe their understanding of the relationship between international relations theory and humanitarian intervention: "Humanitarian intervention is one of the primary international security problems of today. As an object analysis, it sits at the intersection of the realist and idealist traditions in the study of international relations."[20] Dr. David Tucker shares the same sentiment, stating that understanding the middle position between Realism and Idealism "provides the most solid basis we have for deliberating about humanitarian assistance operations."[21]

---

[19] Catherine Toups, "Albright Cites 'Moral Imperative' for Bosnia Mission," *Washington Times*, December 13, 1995, 1.

[20] Mona Fixdal and Dan Smith, "Humanitarian Intervention and Just War," *Mershon International Studies Review* 42, no. 2 (November 1998): 283.

[21] Ambassador Robert B. Oakley and David Tucker, edited by Earl Tilford, Jr., *Two Perspectives on Interventions and Humanitarian Operations* (Carlisle Barracks: Army War College, 1997), 22.

In the case of foreign humanitarian assistance, a Realist would suggest the nation's vital interests are not at stake and the military should not be used to support the operation, especially if doing so puts U.S. military personnel at risk, even inadvertently.[22] The Idealist would suggest the basis of U.S. intervention lies in the simple idealistic desire and the nation's ability to intervene. The Idealist believes the United States' collective moral concerns for global human rights, universal freedoms, and other liberal Western-democracy values usually justifies humanitarian intervention.

John Waghelstein captures this perspective on the two major thrusts of U.S. policy as it is applied to U.S. foreign humanitarian assistance in general, and military assistance in particular:

> There has always been a sort of "two-fers" character to our engagement overseas. First there are *Realpolitik* interests (survival, vital, major and peripheral) that may include over-arching defense considerations, regional stability or access to resources. Second, there is a moral interest, the desire to be in the right—to be on the "side of the angels." Americans have been most comfortable when clear and articulated national interests are coupled with the high moral ground position (e.g. "Save the Union **AND** Free the Slaves"; "Defeat German Militarism **AND** Fight a War to End All Wars")[23]

After gaining an appreciation and understanding of U.S. national interests, one could argue that undertaking foreign humanitarian assistance operations, to include the use of the U.S. military, is within the realm of the United States' interests. This argument is valid if U.S. leaders believe it is the United States' duty and moral responsibility, and therefore in the nation's interest, to provide foreign humanitarian assistance. U.S. leaders must provide strategic guidance and develop policy to guide decisions on behalf of the American people. The guidance should clearly outline why and when the United States

---

[22] Ibid.

[23] John D. Waghelstein, *Military-To-Military Contacts: Personal Observations—The El Salvador Case.* U.S. Military Group, El Salvador Country Team, Fall, 2002, 4.

should use its military in support of foreign humanitarian assistance operations. Absent clear strategic guidance, a dilemma develops in that every foreign humanitarian crisis becomes a requirement to act, and there are no priorities because crisis events will continue to drive interests. Foreign humanitarian assistance decisions should be guided by calculated understanding of national interests and benefits of larger support for international order. To develop an understanding of contemporary strategic guidance a thorough review and analysis of strategies and guidance provided by U.S. national leaders and policymakers follows.

CHAPTER 2

STRATEGIC PERSPECTIVES

This chapter offers a review of strategic guidance to inform the analysis and develop an understanding of contemporary perspectives, strategies, and policies provided by U.S. national leaders. From here, assumptions can be framed regarding national leadership's expected use of the U.S. military to support future foreign humanitarian assistance operations as well as assess the role of the operations in support of U.S. national interests. The review of strategic guidance and analysis will focus on nine specific national level documents that are relevant to this study and collectively form the foundation of U.S. strategy for foreign humanitarian assistance: 2010 U.S. National Security Strategy, Presidential Executive Order 12966, 2012 Defense Strategic Guidance, 2008 National Defense Strategy, 2010 Quadrennial Defense Review, Department of Defense Directive 5100.46, 2011 National Military Strategy, 2010 Department of State Quadrennial Diplomacy and Development Review, and U.S. Senate Bill 3196 from the 112th Congress. Special consideration for guidance relating to military support for foreign humanitarian assistance operations will be provided in the analysis.

U.S. National Security Strategy

The National Security Strategy, authored by President Barack Obama and published in 2010, identifies the major national security concerns and describes the strategic environment the United States desires to shape for tomorrow. This document serves as an overarching strategy for the United States and identifies national security interests. The National Security Strategy deserves careful review as all other government documents and policies should support the interests and objectives listed in the National Security Strategy.

The National Security Strategy begins with a memorandum from President Obama that addresses the fact that "we live in a time of sweeping change"[1] in terms of "accelerated globalization on an unprecedented scale."[2] The memorandum also stresses the need for building coalitions and institutions in the international system to meet the challenges of a new century: "The burdens of a young century cannot fall on American shoulders alone—indeed, our adversaries would like to see America sap our strength by overextending our power."[3]

Relating to humanitarian assistance, the memorandum describes a "commitment to human dignity; support for development and universal rights; resolving and preventing conflict; and helping countries feed themselves and care for their sick."[4] President Obama concludes his preface to the National Security Strategy by describing a movement away from predominate use of military power by stressing that "…security will come not from our ability to instill fear in other peoples, but through our capacity to speak to their hopes. And that work will best be done through the power of the decency and dignity of the American people – our troops and diplomats, but also our private sector, nongovernmental organizations, and citizens."[5] Specific to national interests, the National Security Strategy indicates:

> To achieve the world we seek, the United States must apply our strategic
> approach in pursuit of four enduring national interests." 1) Security: The

---

[1] U.S. President, *National Security Strategy* (Washington DC: Government Printing Office, May 2010): Informantion and quotes in first paragraph of this chapter were taken from President Obama's Memorandum attached to beginning of document, 1.

[2] U.S. President, National Security Strategy, 1.

[3] Ibid., 2.

[4] Ibid.

[5] Ibid., Preface, III.

security of the United States, its citizens, and U.S. allies and partners. 2) Prosperity: A strong, innovative, and growing U.S. economy in an open international economic system that promotes opportunity and prosperity. 3) Values: Respect for universal values at home and around the world. 4) International Order: An international order advanced by U.S. leadership that promotes peace, security, and opportunity through stronger cooperation to meet global challenges.[6]

The National Security Strategy includes several references to foreign humanitarian interests that when collectively considered help provide the United States' strategic approach in pursuit of these interests. The use of the U.S. military, "at times, may be necessary…to preserve broader peace and security, including by protecting civilians facing a grave humanitarian crisis."[7] Highlighting the need to invest in the capacity of strong and capable partners, "the United States…cannot shy away from the difficult task of pursuing stabilization in conflict and post-conflict environments."[8] Elaborating on support to at-risk states, the National Security Strategy indicates that "proactively investing in stronger societies and human welfare is far more effective and efficient than responding after state collapse."[9] President Obama states, "We are increasing our foreign assistance…."[10] When discussing the desire to promote human dignity by meeting basic needs, the National Security Strategy provides specificity in regards to foreign assistance, "the purpose of our foreign assistance will be to create the conditions where it is no longer needed."[11] The document also states, "we will continue to respond to humanitarian crises to ensure that those in need have the protection and assistance they need."[12] Further expanding on humanitarian crisis, "…a changing

---

[6] U.S. President, National Security Strategy, 17.
[7] Ibid, 22.
[8] Ibid., 26.
[9] Ibid., 27.
[10] Ibid., 33.
[11] Ibid., 39.
[12] Ibid., 40.

20

climate portends a future in which the United States must be better prepared and resourced to exercise robust leadership to help meet critical humanitarian needs."[13]

Analysis of the National Security Strategy indicates a hybrid approach using a blend of realism and idealism constructs to outline the nation's security strategy, although an idealist approach largely frames U.S. support for foreign humanitarian assistance operations—with special emphasis on using humanitarian operations to promote U.S. values abroad. Moreover, the contents of the National Security Strategy suggest that one can reasonably assume the U.S. military will be engaged more, not less, to support foreign humanitarian assistance operations—particularly in response to natural disasters. It is important to emphasize that the National Security Strategy promotes a whole of government[14] approach which underscores more than U.S. military involvement in supporting foreign humanitarian assistance operations.

U.S. Presidential Executive Order 12966, Foreign Disaster Assistance

On July 14, 1995 President Clinton signed Executive Order 12966 stating "the Secretary of Defense is hereby directed to provide disaster assistance outside the United States to respond to manmade or natural disasters when the Secretary of Defense determines that such assistance is necessary to prevent loss of lives."[15] This Executive Order clearly articulates to the Department of Defense that disaster assistance, a subset of humanitarian assistance, is an expected and ordered responsibility for the U.S. military. The Executive Order further states, "The Secretary of Defense shall provide disaster assistance only: (a) at the direction of the President; or (b) with the concurrence of the

---

[13] U.S. President, National Security Strategy, 40.
[14] Ibid., 14-16.
[15] U.S. President, Executive Order 12966, "Foreign Disaster Assistance," Published in the *Federal Register* (July 18, 1995).

21

Secretary of State; or (c) in emergency situations in order to save human lives, where there is not sufficient time to seek the prior initial concurrence of the Secretary of State..."[16] President Clinton, by signing Executive Order 12966, formalized his enduring idealist expectation that the United States will use its military to support foreign disaster assistance and thus promote the universal value of life and human dignity.

U.S. Department of Defense Strategic Guidance

In 2012, President Obama directed a Department of Defense review "to identify our strategic interests and guide our defense priorities and spending over the coming decade."[17] The review drove the publication of the U.S. Government's Defense Strategic Guidance—"Sustaining U.S. Global Leadership: Priorities for 21st Century Defense," and was shaped by the four U.S. enduring national interests previously identified in this chapter; security, prosperity, values, and international order. The guidance was influenced by mandated reductions to federal spending required by the Budget Control Act of 2011 and states that "...the Joint Force will need to recalibrate its capabilities and make selective additional investments to succeed in the following missions:

- Counter Terrorism and Irregular Warfare

- Deter and Defeat Aggression

- Project Power Despite Anti-Access/Area Denial Challenges

- Counter Weapons of Mass Destruction

- Operate Effectively in Cyberspace and Space

- Maintain a Safe, Secure, and Effective Nuclear Deterrent

- Defend the Homeland and Provide Support to Civil Authorities

---

[16] U.S. President, Executive Order 12966.
[17] President Barack Obama, *Sustaining U.S. Global Leadership: Priorities for the 21st Century Defense* (Washington DC: Government Printing Office, January 2012).

- Provide a Stabilizing Presence

- Conduct Stability and Counterinsurgency Operations

- Conduct Humanitarian, Disaster Relief, and Other Operations"[18]

Specific to U.S. military support for foreign humanitarian assistance operations, the guidance highlights historically frequent requests for military support and predicts the nation will continue to use the military to protect the safety and well-being of humans throughout the world. Moreover, the guidance reiterates the Department of Defense's position that U.S. military forces are well equipped and "...invaluable in supplementing lead relief agencies, by extending aid to victims of natural or man-made disasters, both at home and abroad."[19] In line with the National Security Strategy, analysis of the Department of Defense's strategic guidance suggests that the U.S. military is postured, and fully expects to be called-on, to support a large number of foreign humanitarian assistance operations.

U.S. National Defense Strategy

The National Defense Strategy was last published in 2008 and is somewhat outdated in its clear assessment of the current strategic environment. However, in context, the National Defense Strategy serves as the Department of Defense's strategic guidance capstone document. The document "also provides a framework for other Department of Defense strategic guidance, specifically on campaign and contingency planning, force development, and intelligence."[20]

---

[18] U.S. Department of Defense, *Sustaining U.S. Global Leadership: Priorities for the 21st Century Defense* (Washington DC: Government Printing Office, January 2012), 4-6.

[19] Ibid., 6.

[20] U.S. Department of Defense, *National Defense Strategy* (Washington DC: Government Printing Office, June 2008), 1-2.

The document outlines five key Department of Defense objectives: Defend the Homeland; Win the Long War; Promote Security; Deter Conflict; and Win our Nation's Wars.[21] Specific to humanitarian assistance, the document highlights that the United States, in pursuit of national interests, has "used diplomacy and soft power [humanitarian assistance] to shape the behavior of individual states and the international system."[22] Describing methods for achieving the objectives, the National Defense Strategy specifies the desire to strengthen and expand alliances and partnerships, "We will be able to rely on many partners for certain low-risk missions such as peacekeeping and humanitarian assistance..."[23] Assessment of the document indicates a strong self-realization, perhaps indicative of the Department of Defense's stress at the time from fighting two wars, that the U.S. military cannot do everything. The document stresses the need for building partnership capacity in other nations and improving interagency cooperation with departments and agencies across the whole of the U.S. Government. The Department of Defense has made significant progress towards this goal since the National Defense Strategy was published over four years ago.

Quadrennial Defense Review Report

The Quadrennial Defense Review, published in 2010, is drafted every four years by the Department of Defense and is an assessment of defense strategy, force structure, weapons programs, and operations designed to guide defense programming, operational planning, and budgets for the overall purpose of protecting the American people and

---

[21] U.S. Department of Defense, *National Defense Strategy*, 6.
[22] Ibid.
[23] Ibid., 15.

advancing national interests.[24] The report reflects two central themes approached by the Department of Defense: 1) rebalance priorities; and 2) reform ways of doing business thus using limited resources more efficiently. Regarding the theme to rebalance priorities, the report identifies the Department of Defense's four priority objectives: 1) prevail in today's wars; 2) prevent and deter conflict; 3) prepare to succeed in a wide range of contingencies, both near- and longer-term; and 4) preserve and enhance the force.[25] Moreover, the report conveys that Department of Defense analysis indicates a need to focus on and improve "six key mission areas:

- Defend the United States and support civil authorities at home;

- Succeed in counterinsurgency, stability, and counterterrorism operations;

- Build the security capacity of partner states;

- Deter and defeat aggression in anti-access environments;

- Prevent proliferation and counter weapons of mass destruction; and

- Operate effectively in cyberspace."[26]

The six key mission areas represent a broad area of joint force responsibilities and reflect the breadth of challenges recognized by the Department of Defense for training, equipping, and employing forces in support of national interests.

With regard to foreign humanitarian assistance, the Quadrennial Defense Review describes the importance of strengthening U.S. Government interagency partnerships and

---

[24] Congressional Research Service, Quadrennial Defense Review 2010: Overview and Implications for national Security Planning, by Stephen Daggett, May 17, 2010 (Washington, DC: Government Printing Office, 2010), 1.

[25] U.S. Department of Defense, *Quadrennial Defense Review Report*, (Washington, DC: Secretary of Defense, February 2010), 17.

[26] U.S. Department of Defense, *Quadrennial Defense Review Report*, 17.

reaffirms support for greater investments in the capabilities of the U.S. Department of

State and U.S. Aid for International Development (USAID):[27]

> Just as maintaining America's enduring defense alliances and relationships
> abroad is a central facet of statecraft, so too is the need to continue
> improving the Department of Defense's cooperation with other U.S.
> departments and agencies. Years of war have proven how important it is
> for America's civilian agencies to possess the resources and authorities
> needed to operate alongside the U.S. Armed Forces during complex
> contingencies at home and abroad. As our experiences in Afghanistan and
> Iraq have shown, sustainable outcomes require civilian development and
> governance experts who can help build local civilian capacity.[28]

The report also reaffirms the Department of Defense's position that foreign humanitarian

assistance operations should be led by non-military organizations: "Although the U.S.

military can and should have the expertise and capacity to conduct these activities,

civilian leadership of humanitarian assistance, development, and governance is

essential."[29]

The Quadrennial Defense Review highlights in several instances requirements for

the U.S. military to support foreign humanitarian operations, such as "it may be in the

U.S. interest to help strengthen weak states, including those…that have been weakened

by humanitarian disasters."[30] Moreover, the report reiterates the need to maintain the

U.S. military's unique capabilities "to create a secure environment in fragile states in

support of local authorities and, if necessary, to support civil authorities in providing

essential government services, restoring emergency infrastructure, and supplying

humanitarian relief."[31] Lastly, in crafting a strategic approach to climate change, the

Department of Defense highlights "…extreme weather events may lead to increased

---

[27] Congressional Research Service, Quadrennial Defense Review 2010: Overview and Implications for national Security Planning, 17.
[28] U.S. Department of Defense, *Quadrennial Defense Review Report*, 69.
[29] Ibid.
[30] U.S. Department of Defense, *Quadrennial Defense Review Report*, 20.
[31] Ibid.

demands for defense support to civil authorities for humanitarian assistance or disaster response both within the United States and overseas."[32]

Department of Defense Directive 5100.46

On July 6, 2012, the Department of Defense reissued Directive 5100.46 to update policy and responsibilities for foreign disaster relief operations in accordance with sections 404 and 2561 of Title 10, United States Code and Executive Order 12966. The document informs Department of Defense agencies on protocols for funding and interagency requests for Department of Defense assistance to disaster relief efforts. The document also prescribes:

> Department of Defense shall consider foreign disaster relief assistance requests from USAID, the Department of State, and other Federal departments and agencies based on USG and/or appropriate international organization assessment(s) of the disaster, the availability of requested assistance, the impact on ongoing or potential military operations of providing such assistance, the effect on security cooperation objectives, and other relevant factors associated with Department of Defense involvement.[33]

In support of Executive Order 12966, the Directive provides additional specificity to U.S. military commanders in regard to providing prompt foreign disaster relief assistance: "Nothing in this Directive shall be construed as preventing a military commander with assigned forces at or near the immediate scene of a foreign disaster from taking prompt action to save human lives."[34] The Directive also outlines specific responsibilities pertaining to supporting foreign disaster relief operations for Department of Defense agencies, military services, and commanders of combatant commands.

U.S. National Military Strategy

---

[32] Ibid., 85.
[33] U.S. Department of Defense, *Directive 5100.46: Foreign Disaster Relief (FDR)*, July 6, 2012 (Washington DC: Department of Defense, 6 July 2012), 2.
[34] Ibid.

The National Military Strategy, authored by the Chairman of the Joint Chiefs of Staff, was published in 2011. The purpose of the document is to provide the ways and means by which the U.S. military will advance enduring national interests as described in President Obama's 2010 National Security Strategy, as well as accomplish the Department of Defense objectives outlined in the 2010 Quadrennial Defense Review. The National Military Strategy is "derived from a thorough assessment of the strategic environment and how to advance our national interests within it."[35]

In describing the strategy for the national military objective to "Strengthen International and Regional security," the document provides specific inferences to U.S. military support for foreign humanitarian assistance:

> We must plan and exercise extensively across the Combatant Commanders' seams of responsibility for full spectrum contingencies to support U.S. diplomatic and development efforts and help mitigate and contain the human and economic impact of crisis. Humanitarian assistance and disaster relief activities employ the Joint Force to address partner needs and sometimes provide opportunities to build confidence and trust between erstwhile adversaries. They also help us gain and maintain access and relationships that support our broader national interests. We must be prepared to support and facilitate the response of USAID and other U.S. government agencies' to humanitarian crisis.[36]

Analysis of the National Military Strategy indicates the U.S. military fully expects to be called on by national leaders to support foreign humanitarian assistance operations, ranging from disaster relief crisis response actions to supporting and enforcing human rights, even in sometimes hostile situations. The National Military Strategy also indicates that foreign humanitarian assistance operations help the United States "gain and

---

[35] Chairman of the Joint Chiefs of Staff, *The National Military Strategy of the United States of America* (Washington DC: Department of Defense, February 2011), 21.

[36] Chairman of the Joint Chiefs of Staff, The National Military Strategy of the United States of America, 15.

maintain" access that can in-turn support national security interests with higher levels of intensity.

Review and analysis of strategic guidance through the lens of the military element of national power indicates that national leaders, from the President to the Secretary of Defense, fully support and even raise a level of expectation for using the U.S. military to advance U.S. national interests operating in support of foreign humanitarian assistance operations. The research and analysis will continue by looking through the lens of the diplomatic element of national power.

Quadrennial Diplomacy and Development Review

The U.S. Department of State published the first-ever Quadrennial Diplomacy and Development Review in 2010 as a strategy to implement a reform agenda for the State Department and USAID. Secretary of State Hillary Clinton initiated development of the document as a precursor to elevating civilian power alongside military power as an equal, if not leading, pillar of U.S. foreign policy, described as the "Three Ds:" diplomacy, development, and defense. The document acknowledges the State Department's desire to become a more capable element of national power:

> To realize the full potential of civilian power, to give the U.S. military the partner it needs and deserves, and to advance U.S. national interests around the world, U.S. foreign policy structures and processes must adapt to the 21st century. The President's commitment to "whole-of-government" must be more than a mantra.[37]

Secretary Clinton also "called for an integrated "smart power" approach to solving global problems—a concept that is embodied in the President's National Security Strategy."[38]

The Quadrennial Diplomacy and Development Review is organized into five

---

[37] U.S. Secretary of State. *Quadrennial Diplomacy and Development Review* (Washington DC: Department of State, 2010), 4.
[38] Ibid., ii.

chapters: 1) Global Trends and Guiding Principles, 2) Adapting to the Diplomatic Landscape of the 21st Century, 3) Elevating and Transforming Development to Deliver Results, 4) Preventing and Responding to Crisis, Conflict and Instability, and 5) Working Smarter.[39] The document identifies humanitarian assistance as one of six specific areas for USAID to focus development efforts. Underscoring the point that USAID is the U.S. Government's lead development agency, the document also highlights the need for partners across the government, including the U.S. military:

> As we saw recently in Haiti, USAID's cooperation with the Department of Defense can be important to ensuring rapid humanitarian assistance in large scale disasters, where the military's transportation, logistics, and engineering capabilities are critical. Our approach going forward values these contributions and seeks great alignment and collaboration among these development partners.[40]

Further elaborating that humanitarian assistance is a whole of government undertaking, the document states, "How efficiently State and USAID work together and with other U.S. government agencies bears directly on lives and human suffering, and ultimately, a country's ability to return to a path of enduring growth and development."[41] Described as one of State Department's "comparative strengths," the document highlights humanitarian assistance as a diplomatic focus area where the United States can have the greatest impact:

> When disaster strikes—whether floods in Pakistan or an earthquake in Haiti—the United States has always responded to the call for help. And our diplomats, development professionals, and military have the capability to answer that call as no other nation can. For both moral and strategic reasons we will continue to do so, building and focusing on our comparative strengths. This way, we will make certain that when other

---

[39] Ibid., 07-08.
[40] U.S. Secretary of State. *Quadrennial Diplomacy and Development Review*, 78.
[41] Ibid., 91.

nations face their day of need, America responds with swift, meaningful aid that reflects the full measure of our compassion.[42]

The Quadrennial Diplomacy and Development Review reflects the ideological nature of the current Presidential administration and indicates that foreign humanitarian assistance is a key aspect of the United States' development pillar of foreign policy. The document stresses the need for a "whole of government" approach to support foreign humanitarian assistance operations and highlights the requirement for U.S. military support to provide capabilities not inherent in the State Department nor USAID, such as transportation, logistics, and engineering support. In step with the National Security Strategy and Department of Defense strategic documents, the Quadrennial Diplomacy and Development Review indicates that one can reasonably assume the U.S. military will continue be regularly engaged to support foreign humanitarian assistance operations.

U.S. Senate Bill 3176, Military Humanitarian Operations Act of 2012

U.S. support for foreign humanitarian assistance is a key interest of national leaders and remains a point of discussion in the contemporary political environment. Some leaders, from an idealist perspective, believe the United States should lean favorably towards supporting foreign humanitarian requests; yet others, from a realist perspective, suggest the United States should proceed more cautiously. Recognizing the seriousness of committing the U.S. military to support foreign humanitarian assistance operations, sometimes in hostile environments that put Americans at risk, Senators Jim Webb and Mike Lee submitted a bill on May 14, 2012 to the 112th Congress, to place control measures on committing the U.S. military for such operations. The bill, cited as the "Military Humanitarian Operations Act of 2012" states: "To provide that the

---

[42] U.S. Secretary of State. Quadrennial Diplomacy and Development Review, 90.

President must seek congressional approval before engaging members of the United

States Armed Forces in military humanitarian operations."[43] The proposed Act defines

the term "military humanitarian operation" as:

> A military operation involving the deployment of members or weapon
> systems of the United States Armed Forces where hostile activities are
> reasonably anticipated and with the aim of preventing or responding to a
> humanitarian catastrophe, including its regional consequences, or
> addressing a threat posed to international peace and security.[44]

The proposed Act further states the term includes all operations undertaken in support of

the United Nations Security Council or other unilateral deployments made in

coordination with "international organizations, treaty-based organizations, or coalitions

formed to address specific humanitarian catastrophes."[45] Further, the proposed Act

describes the legislative procedures that would be used to quickly debate and procedures

to vote on the President's request to use the U.S. military to support the specified foreign

humanitarian assistance operation. The bill was read twice and referred to the Committee

on Foreign Relations on May 14, 2012. At the time of this study there were no Roll Call

votes for the bill.

Although the bill has not moved beyond the Committee on Foreign Relations in

the Congress, it remains relevant for the purpose of this study as the bill highlights a

premise shared by some national leaders that the United States should not commit the

U.S. military to support foreign humanitarian assistance operations without deliberate and

meaningful debate. A contingent of national leaders, like Senators Webb and Lee, share

a realist perspective that although the United States may sense a moral imperative to use

its military to support foreign humanitarian assistance operations, it should not

---

[43] *Military Humanitarian Operations Act of 2012*, S3176, 112th Cong., 2d sess. (May 14, 2012), 1.
[44] Ibid., 2.
[45] *Military Humanitarian Operations Act of 2012*, S3176, 112th Cong., 2d sess. (May 14, 2012), 2.

necessarily act on that moral imperative unless the military action aligns with national interests. This initiative indicates the desire of some members of Congress to validate military support with national interests, not just the President. The premise highlights a political conundrum in that the President defines the nation's interests through the National Security Strategy which is submitted to Congress. Yet as Commander in Chief, the President can be limited in the deployment of military forces by the Congress as stated in the U.S. Constitution. Additionally the President, as commander in chief, has authority from Congress per the War Powers Act of 1973 to deploy military assets without Congressional approval, although traditionally the President will confer with Congress or notify them before doing so. A June 29, 2011 *New York Times* article provides historical context of the War Powers Act:

> In practice, more power has lodged in the White House than on Capitol Hill. Scholars have estimated that presidents have dispatched forces abroad between 120 and 200 times, but Congress has only formally declared war on five occasions: the War of 1812, the Spanish-American War, the Mexican-American War and the two World Wars…
> The Law requires the president to notify Congress in a timely fashion when American troops are being sent abroad with a strong probability that they will engage in combat. It calls for the troops to be removed from foreign territory within 60 days unless Congress explicitly gives approval for them to remain.[46]

The 60 day restriction is a key aspect and is interpreted by most Presidential administrations, regardless of political affiliation, as an infringement upon the President as commander in chief. The President may have the authority to deploy forces (by exception without prior approval of Congress) but the President is limited in the duration of that deployment, however initiated by

---

[46] Author not listed on Opinion/Editorial column, "War Powers Act of 1973," *The New York Times*, June 29, 2011, http://topics.nytimes.com/top/reference/timestopics/subjects/w/war_powers_act_of_1973/index.html (accessed February 23, 2013).

Congress. Historically Congress has been sporadic in the enforcement of this constraint.

Specific to military support for foreign humanitarian support operations, Senate Bill 3176 appears as an attempt to rectify the apparent disparity between the intent of the War Powers Act of 1973. Moreover, the bill aims to limit the ability of the President to engage in major combat operations and recent administrations' initiatives to commit the military to support humanitarian assistance operations which later turned into major combat operations. An alternative course of action to rectify the disparity would be for Congress to initiate an amendment to the War Powers Act and add similar language to the Act as described in Senate Bill 3176.

In summary, the review and analysis of contemporary strategic guidance suggests that U.S. leaders and policymakers fully expect the U.S. military to be involved in future foreign humanitarian support operations. U.S. strategy can be largely categorized as idealistic in terms of supporting foreign humanitarian assistance to promote U.S. values abroad, although the U.S. strategy hints at a realistic approach when it describes using foreign humanitarian assistance to gain access in support of broader U.S. objectives. National strategy falls short by failing to provide specificity in terms of U.S. military involvement in foreign humanitarian assistance operations conducted in non-permissive or hostile environments, although arguably it may be difficult to craft specificity to which exception would be found almost routinely. Analysis of strategic guidance highlights the classic dichotomy between military and political mindsets: clarity versus ambiguity.

The next two chapters of this study will present historical case studies of U.S. military involvement in foreign humanitarian assistance operations during the Berlin Airlift (1948-1949) and Somalia (1992-1994). The Berlin Airlift will provide an illustration of using a realist political approach to achieve U.S. national security interests using military soft power to support foreign humanitarian assistance operations. Conversely, a review of U.S. military intervention in Somalia, dampened by political challenges, will illustrate an idealist political approach where military activities in support of foreign humanitarian assistance operations did not fully support U.S. national security interests. Analysis of the case studies will provide a historical perspective to help establish a basis for recommendations to define parameters for U.S. leaders and policymakers to consider when linking U.S. military involvement in foreign humanitarian assistance operations to U.S. national security interests.

CHAPTER 3

THE BERLIN AIRLIFT 1948-1949

The Berlin Airlift…an incredible feat wherein an entire city was totally
supplied from the air. Probably in no other case has the military played so
vital a humanitarian role. More than any other event, the images of those
planes delivering everything from food to coal fostered acceptance of the
link between [military] air forces and humanitarian assistance…[1]

At the end of World War II, Germany was divided into four zones, each occupied

and controlled by one of four Allied victors. The Soviet Union controlled the Eastern

half of Germany while France, Great Britain, and the United States divided and

controlled the Western half of the country. Berlin, the capital city and symbolic center of

political power and German culture, was located in the heart of the Soviet Union's zone

and isolated from Western Allies.[2] Berlin was also divided into four sectors. The Soviet

Union controlled East Berlin, and the free sectors of West Berlin were divided and

occupied by France, Britain and the United States.

On June 23, 1948 the Soviet Union released the following message announcing

the complete suspension of railway, road and canal access through any portions of

Soviet-controlled East Germany:

> Transport Division of the Soviet Military Administration is compelled to
> halt all passenger and freight traffic to and from Berlin tomorrow at 0600
> hours because of technical difficulties. It is impossible to reroute traffic in
> the interests of maintaining rail service, since such measures would
> unfavorably affect the entire railroad traffic in the Soviet Occupation
> Zone.[3]

---

[1] Frederick C. Cuny, "Use of the Military in Humanitarian Relief," speech given at Niinsalo, Finland
Military Academy, November, 1989, "Frontline, PBS Online.
http://www.pbs.org/wgbh/pages/frontline/shows/cuny/laptop/humanrelief html (accessed September 9, 2012), 1.

[2] David G. Estep, *Air Mobility: The Strategic Use of Nonlethal Airpower* (Maxwell AFB, AL: Air University,
1994), 16.

[3] Frank Donovan, *Bridge in the Sky* (New York: David McKay Company Inc., 1968), 36.

The Soviets followed with a second message the same day that left no doubt about Soviet intentions to isolate the entire city:

> Water traffic will be suspended. Coal shipments from the Soviet Zone are halted. The Soviet authorities have also ordered the central switching stations to stop the supply of electric power from the Soviet Zone and the Soviet Sector to the Western Sector. Shortage of coal to operate the plants is the reason.[4]

As a result Berlin became a besieged city, with 2.25 million people facing potential starvation and a freezing winter season without coal and oil for heating. The only Soviet-permitted access to Berlin consisted of three 20-mile wide air corridors from Western Germany to the Tempelhof and Gatow airports located within the British and American sectors of Berlin. The Soviet Union believed the blockade would force the Western Allies from Berlin and set the conditions for expansion of Soviet-backed communism. An opening salvo of the Cold War, the blockade presented the United States with a decision that would determine the future of U.S.—Soviet Union relations.[5]

Historical Background, National Interests, Strategic Decisions

Prior to the Berlin blockade, the United States was about to realize significant national interests in Germany and throughout all of war-torn Europe, including the development of a free-market economic system based on free enterprise and support for national governments anchored in parliamentary democracies. In light of these interests, the United States implemented the European Recovery Program, commonly referred to as the Marshall Plan, to provide extensive reconstruction and economic aid to help rebuild European economies and create economic growth in Europe. Moreover, the Truman Doctrine was announced as the United States' policy for "containing" communism. On

---

[4] Frank Donovan, *Bridge in the Sky* (New York: David McKay Company Inc., 1968), 36.
[5] Estep, *Air Mobility: The Strategic Use of Nonlethal Airpower*, 17.

March 12, 1947, President Harry S. Truman, in a declaration to the U.S. Congress stated, "I believe that it must be the policy of the United States to support free peoples who are resisting attempted subjugation by armed minorities or outside pressures."[6]

The Soviet Union believed the U.S. policies were nothing more than a ploy by the United States to dominate Europe through political, economic and cultural penetration. The final action, viewed by the Soviet Union as a provocation, transpired in June 1948 when the Western Allies announced their intention to issue the western German Deutsch mark to the western sectors of Berlin. The Soviets asserted the currency reform was illegal and part of a scheme to permanently divide Germany. Soviet retaliation quickly materialized into the Berlin blockade and the United States faced a decision to support the largest foreign humanitarian assistance operation in its history.

General Lucius Clay, the U.S. Commander in Chief, European Command (CINCEUR), and Military Governor of Germany was not totally surprised by the Soviet blockade. In a letter sent to Washington D.C. in April of 1948, two months prior to the blockade, he highlighted the importance of maintaining a U.S. presence in Berlin:

> We have lost Czechoslovakia. Norway is threatened. We retreat from
> Berlin. When Berlin falls, western Germany will be next. If we mean…to
> hold Europe against Communism, we must not budge. We can take
> humiliation and pressure short of war in Berlin without losing face. If we
> withdraw, our position in Europe is threatened. If America does not
> understand this now, does not know that the issue is cast, then it never will
> and communism will run rampant. I believe the future of democracy
> requires us to stay.[7]

President Truman agreed with General Clay's assessment and understood the strategic importance of the blockade in that the balance of power in Europe hinged on the rise of democracy, or conversely, the rise of communism in Berlin. President Truman

---

[6] Eric Morris, *Blockade: Berlin and the Cold War* (New York: Stein and Day, 1973), 79.
[7] Lucius D. Clay, *Decision in Germany* (New York: Double Day & Co., 1950), 361.

believed that Soviet influence, if allowed to expand in Berlin, would likely continue to permeate throughout Germany, and possibly make all of Europe vulnerable over time if left unchecked. Accordingly, President Truman vowed to maintain the prestige and influence of the Western Allies in Germany and his response to the blockade was "guided by the thought that U.S. vital national security interests were at stake in Europe."[8]

President Truman led the United States and Western Allies in resisting Soviet expansion by using military power in terms of airlift to execute humanitarian assistance operations in Berlin. The airlift supported Berlin's humanitarian requirements while affording the United States and Western Allies time for diplomacy to resolve the conflict with the Soviet Union. General Clay articulated the United States' resolve for continued U.S. military support for the Berlin airlift:

> There is no practicability in maintaining our position in Berlin and it must not be evaluated on that basis…We are convinced that our remaining in Berlin is essential to our prestige in Germany and in Europe. Whether for good or bad, it has become a symbol of American intent.[9]

On June 25, 1948, General Clay ordered General Curtis Lemay, Commander of U.S. Air Forces in Europe, to commence the airlift, identified as Operation Vittles. The Airlift Task Force, initially commanded by Major General Joseph Smith, used 102 C-47 Skytrain and two C-54 Skymaster aircraft that were immediately available in the European theater to commence operations.[10] Berlin imported 15,500 tons of material daily before the Soviet blockade, and although requirements were not precise initially, the estimate for Berlin's survival was

---

[8] Estep, Air Mobility: The Strategic Use of Nonlethal Airpower, 17.
[9] Gregory C. Tine, "Berlin Airlift: Logistics, Humanitarian Aid, and Strategic Success," *Army Logistician* 37, no. 5, September/October 2005, 39.
[10] William H. Tunner, *Over the Hump* (New York: Duall, Sloan and Pearce, 1964), 158.

4,000 tons a day.[11] Within three weeks Operation Vittles delivered approximately

1,500 tons of material a day, while the British were contributing an additional 750

tons a day.[12] Despite these impressive results, the effort demonstrated Allied

resolve but was inadequate for the long term sustainment of Berlin.

In July, 1948 President Truman reaffirmed the United States' long-term

commitment to Berlin, and as a result, drove the requirement for more expertise

and resources to support the Berlin Airlift. Major General William Tunner,

Deputy Commander of the Military Air Transport Service (MATS), was selected

to run the airlift. General Tunner was an expert in airlift operations due to his

experience from flying operations over the "Hump" from India to China during

World War II. The U.S. Air Force also committed additional aircraft to Operation

Vittles, including MATS-assigned C-54s from Alaska, Hawaii and the United

States. The C-54 aircraft, more capable and efficient than C-47s, could airlift 10

tons and be loaded in the same amount of time as C-47 aircraft that had less than

three tons of capacity.[13]

General Tunner and his staff quickly improved the efficiency and

effectiveness of Operation Vittles by streamlining pilot and aircraft scheduling,

improving aircraft maintenance practices and cargo handling procedures, and

revamping air traffic control procedures. Operation Vittles was transformed

during the summer of 1948 "from a temporary measure to an operation that was to

---

[11] Tunner, *Over the Hump*, 159.
[12] Ibid., 160.
[13] Ibid., 158.

supply the entire needs of the city of Berlin for an indeterminate period of time."[14]

The Berlin Airlift continued successfully for the remainder of 1948 and through the spring of 1949, despite almost overwhelming obstacles, including adverse weather, aircrew and aircraft fatigue, Soviet aerial harassments, radio beacon jamming, as well as saturated, dangerous flying corridors. Despite the obstacles, Operation Vittles was a success and the Soviets started to realize it. In April, 1949, General Tunner planned a massive single-day airlift to demonstrate Allied resolve to the Soviet Union, "We'd have an Easter Parade of airplanes, and Easter Sunday present for the people of Berlin!"[15] The "Easter Parade" was a resounding success; 1,398 airlift missions were safely flown, delivering 12,941 tons of materiel to Berlin in one day.[16] Throughout the entire Berlin Airlift, Allied aircraft flew 276,926 flights and delivered 2,323,067 tons of materiel to Berlin.

Conclusions and Lessons Learned

Thomas Snyder, Command Historian for U.S. Air Forces in Europe, offers his perspective regarding the significance of the operation in relation to U.S. strategic interests:

> In retrospect, the Berlin Airlift accomplished much more than the delivery of humanitarian assistance. Politically, it galvanized American commitment to European freedom, stability, and security. Tactically, it demonstrated the ability to use [military] airpower to further national policy by peaceful means.[17]

---

[14] Estep, Air Mobility: The Strategic Use of Nonlethal Airpower, 24.
[15] Tunner, *Over the Hump*, 219.
[16] Ibid., 222.
[17] Thomas S. Snyder in the Foreward section of booklet, a reprint of the chapter entitled "Berlin Airlift" from Lieutenant General William H. Tunner's autobiography, *Over the Hump* (Ramstein Air Base: Office of History, U.S. Air Forces in Europe, 1998).

Lasting nearly eleven months, the Soviets ended the blockade of Berlin on May 12, 1949, although humanitarian airlift operations continued until September 30, 1949 in order to build up a surplus of supplies in Berlin. During this time, the United States pursued vital national security interests, maintained prestige in Europe, and demonstrated tremendous resolve against the Soviet Union's attempt to expand communism throughout Germany. General Clay later summarized his thoughts regarding the Berlin Airlift:

> The success of the European Recovery Program [Marshall Plan] and the planned formation of West German Government led to the Soviet blockade of Berlin, a ruthless attempt to use starvation to drive out the Western Powers, thus re-creating in Europe the fear which favored Communist expansion. The airlift prevented the blockade from accomplishing its purpose. There were risks involved in our determination not to be driven out of the former German capital. We understood and accepted these risks… To do so was essential if we were to maintain the cause of freedom. The firm stand of the Western Powers in undertaking the airlift not only prevented terror from again engulfing Europe, but also convinced its free people of our intent to hold our position until peace is assured.[18]

What does examination of the Berlin Airlift indicate in terms of lessons learned for the U.S. military and its activities in support of foreign humanitarian assistance operations in the 21st century? The Berlin Airlift provides a positive and powerful historical illustration of U.S. leaders pursuing a realist approach in terms of using the U.S. military to support clearly defined national security interests. The United States used military power in direct support of national security interests that President Truman deemed vital to the national security of the United States. The President and U.S. national leaders clearly understood that long-term U.S. national security interests in Germany and all of Europe were at stake and that Soviet communism had to be contained in Berlin. The Berlin Airlift illustrated that U.S. military support for foreign

---

[18] Lucius D. Clay, *Decision in Germany* (New York: Double Day & Co., 1950), x.

humanitarian assistance can be a useful means to pursue U.S. national security interests as well as political objectives.

The case study of the Berlin Airlift also illustrates the dual character of U.S. military engagement overseas that was previously discussed in this study.[19] The Berlin Airlift supported U.S. national interests in terms of regional security and the containment of communism, but also supported a high moral ground approach that supported U.S. values. The overwhelming success of the Berlin Airlift, in terms of political and military impact, validates the realist perspective that U.S. military involvement in foreign humanitarian assistance operations can serve larger national interests rather than just simply satisfy the moral or humanitarian crisis at hand. The Berlin Airlift also illustrates the significance of using foreign humanitarian assistance to influence the hearts and minds of local populations, and by doing so, enabled the United States to establish a higher moral ground and achieve a broader strategic purpose in terms of supporting national interests by promoting U.S. values—values the Unites States believes are enduring and universal. Articulated in the President's National Security Strategy, "these values include an individual's freedom to speak their mind, assemble without fear, worship as they please, and choose their own leaders; they also include dignity, tolerance, and equality among all people, and the fair and equitable administration of justice."[20]

The next case study will examine the United States' military involvement in Somalia from 1992-1994 supporting foreign humanitarian assistance operations to relieve widespread starvation and famine that was causing the deaths of thousands of Somalis. The study will illustrate how the United States shifted after the Cold War from primarily

---

[19] John D. Waghelstein, *Military-To-Military Contacts: Personal Observations—The El Salvador Case.* U.S. Military Group, El Salvador Country Team, Fall, 2002, 4.

[20] U.S. President. *National Security Strategy.* Washington DC: Government Printing Office, May 2010, 35.

an interest-based foreign policy to one that rested more on values—a transformation, in essence, from realism to idealism. With the collapse of the Soviet Union and with Saddam Hussein contained from Operations Desert Storm/Desert Shield, the United States lacked an existential threat and subsequently embarked on an ill-defined "new world order." The United States had a plethora of national capacity and power but perhaps lacked a well-defined national strategy that guided the idealistic use of the capacity and power. Analysis of the U.S. intervention in Somalia, aggravated by internal Somali conflict and escalating United Nation political goals, will illustrate an idealist approach where U.S. military involvement in foreign humanitarian assistance operations did not fully support U.S. national security interests.

CHAPTER 4

SOMALIA CASE STUDY

President George Bush's decision to intervene in Somalia in December 1992 may have been his final attempt to demonstrate U.S. support for a new world order. The method he chose, however, raises serious questions about his administration's criteria for intervention. Indeed, critics have denounced it as a formula for failure.[1]

The United States used military force to intervene in Somalia from 1992 to 1994 to assist the United Nations in providing foreign humanitarian assistance in an attempt to resolve widespread starvation and famine. Examination of U.S. military operations in Somalia provides historical context of the U.S. intervention and illustrates the challenges of pursuing foreign humanitarian assistance operations from an idealist perspective. The case study also highlights U.S. leaders' naïve attempt to initially ignore the political aspects of the humanitarian crisis and presents the inherent challenges subsequently faced by the United States while attempting to maintain political neutrality in the midst of an ongoing civil war. Moreover, the United States' involvement in Somalia presents lessons learned that can be useful in identifying parameters for U.S. national leaders and policymakers to consider before committing the U.S. military to support foreign humanitarian assistance operations.

Historical Background, National Interests, Strategic Decisions

Somalia's recent turbulent history began in 1969 when a coalition of army and police officers called the Supreme Revolutionary Council, led by Major General Mohamed Siad Barre, seized power of the national government in a bloodless coup. The Supreme Revolutionary Council assumed all executive and legislative powers in Somalia

---

[1] Lester H. Brune, *The United States and Post-Cold War Interventions, Bush and Clinton in Somalia, Haiti and Bosnia, 1992-1998* (Claremont, CA: Regina Books, 1998), 13.

and later nationalized several foreign companies. Siad Barre and his authoritarian regime remained in power until January 1991 when the political and social situation deteriorated and the regime was ousted by brutal and deadly opposition groups.[2] A civil war ensued and much of the fighting took place in the primary grain-growing region in central-south Somalia. Farmers abandoned their crops and grain production, already hampered by extreme drought conditions, virtually stopped. Foreign aid of mainly food deliveries was used by the warring factions as an instrument of war, with "each faction claiming them for its own supporters and using force to deny food to others."[3] Extreme fighting and clan brutality, coupled with massive famine and starvation, resulted in an estimated 300,000 people dead and was generating a death rate of approximately 3,000 daily with 1.5 million more Somalis at risk.[4]

The United Nations, reacting to the escalating crisis, approved Resolution 751 in April 1992, which authorized humanitarian assistance operations and established the United Nations Operations in Somalia (UNOSOM). A small United Nations peacekeeping force was deployed to Somalia to protect international relief efforts, but the efforts proved largely ineffective as fighting continued amongst the clans and food deliveries continued to be diverted from the starving population.[5]

President Bush, facing increasing domestic and international pressure to assist with the humanitarian crisis, ordered the U.S. military to commence Operation Provide Relief in August 1992. The U.S. Joint Chiefs of Staff had warned the President about "the danger of being drawn into an open-ended commitment," so the operation was

---

[2] Ambassador Robert B. Oakley and David Tucker, edited by Earl Tilford, Jr., *Two Perspectives on Interventions and Humanitarian Operations* (Carlisle Barracks: Army War College, 1997), 1.

[3] Ibid.

[4] Ibid.

[5] Carol D. Clair, *Humanitarian Assistance and the Elements of Operational Design* (Fort Leavenworth, KS: School of Advanced Studies, 1993), 25.

designed primarily as a logistical operation, absent any intended use of force, to help the humanitarian assistance relief effort while minimizing risk to U.S. military personnel.[6] The operation directed the U.S. military to commence foreign humanitarian assistance using U.S Air Force C-130s to airlift food and supplies from Kenya to remote airfields in the interior of Somalia. The airlift operations bypassed congested seaports and reduced the requirement for convoys that were being looted by the warring Somali clans and lawless gangs. International relief organizations, already established in Somalia, continued the ground distribution of the aid from the Somali airfields.

Despite 28,000 tons of food being delivered over a 4-month period, Operation Provide Relief was insufficient in relieving famine across Somalia. Meanwhile 500 Pakistani United Nations peacekeeping forces deployed to Somalia in September 1992, but proved unsuccessful at securing food deliveries. By November 1992, it was clear that UNOSOM and Operation Provide Relief fell short of providing sufficient relief to the Somalis.

Facing increased international pressure to relieve rampant human suffering and also determining the situation in Somalia constituted a threat to international peace and security, the United Nations Security Council passed Resolution 794 in December 1992. Under Resolution 794, the United Nations had expanded its "traditional role of Chapter VI peacekeeping operations to a more ambitious Chapter VII peace enforcement intervention…authorizing participating states of the coalition to use 'all necessary means' to execute the parameters of mandates."[7] Resolution 794 authorized military forces to

---

[6] Walter S. Poole, *The Effort to Save Somalia, August 1992-March 1994* (Washington DC: Joint History Office, Office of the Joint Chiefs of Staff, 2005), 1.

[7] U.S. Army. *United States Forces, Somalia After Action Report and Historical Overview: The United States Army in Somalia, 1992-1994.* (Washington DC: Center for Military History, U.S. Army, 2003), 23.

conduct offensive operations, if required, to establish a secure environment for humanitarian assistance operations in Somalia. Resolution 794, in essence, endorsed imminent U.S.-led security and peacekeeping operations in Somalia and gave the operations legitimacy and an international flavor.

In response to Resolution 794, President Bush authorized a U.S.-led Unified Task Force (UNITAF) and launched Operation Restore Hope in December 1992, one month before he was to leave office and turnover national strategy to the opposing political party. The President ordered deployment of 28,000 U.S. ground forces to Somalia as part of a multilateral response "to address a major humanitarian calamity, avert related threats to international peace and security, and protect the safety of Americans and others engaged in relief operations."[8] President Bush did not indicate any U.S. national security interests in Somalia, although he envisioned Operation Restore Hope as a deliberate operation to protect the existing humanitarian assistance operations in Somalia. Lester Brune in *The United States and Post-Cold War Interventions* describes the absence of U.S. national interests in Somalia: "Television supplied a moral imperative and the public support for Bush's decision to intervene, but the U.S.'s national interest was not directly involved because stabilizing Somalia's political order was not critical to America's economic or political well being."[9]

The initial plans for Operation Restore Hope were based upon the Weinberger-Powell doctrine, which "calls for the use of overwhelming force at the outset in pursuit of a clearly defined and limited mission."[10] Also in-line with the Weinberger-Powell

---

[8] President George Bush, "Humanitarian Crisis in Somalia," *U.S. Department of State Dispatch*, December 14, 1992, 877.
[9] Brune, *The United States and Post-Cold War Interventions*, 20.
[10] Oakley, Tucker and Tilford, 3.

doctrine, Operation Restore Hope was to remain focused solely on its humanitarian assistance mission in order to withdrawal U.S. combat units from Somalia as soon as possible and quickly transfer responsibility from UNITAF to UNOSOM.[11] Brune summarizes the U.S. political environment at the time:

> A moral imperative acceptable to the American public had become evident by November 1992 but because the administration perceived no national interest at stake in Somalia, President Bush seriously qualified the role of the U.S.'s mission. His adoption of a strictly humanitarian mission resulted in the proverbial wrong intervention, in the wrong place, at the wrong time.[12]

President Bush, adamant about limiting the U.S. military's role in Somalia, indicated in a letter to the Speaker of the House and the President Pro Tempore of the Senate: "While it is not possible to estimate precisely how long the transfer of responsibility may take, we believe that prolonged operations will not be necessary."[13]

UNITAF was largely successful at reducing attacks against humanitarian assistance operations during the initial stages of Operation Restore Hope. Understanding the President's intent to avoid violent confrontation, UNITAF forces largely refrained from engaging in armed conflict with the warring factions of militia. U.S. Ambassador Robert Oakley, maintaining that UNITAF forces were ostensibly neutral and only in Somalia to ensure the safety of humanitarian assistance operations, effectively established a cease-fire between the two predominate warlords: General Muhammad Farah Aideed of the Habr Gidr sub clan and Ali Mahdi Mohamed of the Abgal sub-clan in Mogadishu. Aideed and Ali Mahdi feared that U.S. forces would destroy them if

---

[11] Poole, *The Effort to Save Somalia*, 2.
[12] Brune, *The United States and Post-Cold War Interventions*, 13.
[13] Bush, "Humanitarian Crisis in Somalia," 877.

necessary as both warlords knew of the overwhelming firepower of U.S. armed forces.

Ambassador Oakley offered his premise of the situation:

> The United States was convinced that despite its own military superiority, the Somalis would fight rather than give up all their weapons under external coercion. Complete disarmament of all the factions would have required at least a doubling of the UNITAF personnel and, almost certainly, would have resulted in substantial casualties, as well as a disruption of humanitarian operations.[14]

Considering the second order effects of negotiating the cease-fire, in retrospect, Brune suggests that Ambassador Oakley's dealings with Aideed and Ali Mahdi "gave them the appearance of being Somalia's legitimate rulers because he concentrated on the domains of these two Mogadishu leaders."[15]

By the end of December 1992, UNITAF had secured critical geographic objectives in an effort to improve security in Somalia. From January to April 1993, despite some operational setbacks, Operation Restore Hope succeeded in its goal of protecting humanitarian assistance operations and alleviating mass starvation and famine in Somalia. Although UNITAF's humanitarian assistance task was largely accomplished, security steadily eroded and it was ultimately recognized that "lasting peace in Somalia could only be achieved by disarming the warlords and assisting in the restoration of basic social order and societal infrastructure."[16] The President and U.S. military leaders had believed Operation Restore Hope offered a clear exit strategy, but in retrospect, it appears they did not fully understand the "true nature of UNOSOM's troubles, nor the vital

---

[14] Oakley, Tucker and Tilford, 10.

[15] Brune, *The United States and Post-Cold War Interventions*, 24.

[16] U.S. Army. *United States Forces, Somalia After Action Report*, 25.

connection between Somalia's political anarchy and the attainment of success for their "humanitarian" mission."[17]

In March 1993, the United Nations Security Council passed Resolution 814, authorizing the creation of United Nations Organization in Somalia II (UNOSOM II) to assume control of coalition forces in Somalia. Resolution 814 tasked UNOSOM II with the ambitious task to disarm the factions and reach a political settlement by force if necessary, although the resolution was unclear on the issue of coercive disarmament and failed to clearly define an achievable end state for UNOSOM II forces.[18] The United Nations, in essence, was propagating strategy for the international community in terms of dealing with Somali issues.

Before UNOSOM II commenced operations, the United Nations Secretary General requested that U.S.-led UNITAF forcibly disarm all factions, seize heavy weapons, and force some kind of political settlement. The United States, satisfied with the results of Operation Restore Hope by establishing the conditions necessary for humanitarian assistance operations, sensed "mission creep" and rejected the Secretary General's approach. UNITAF subsequently turned over operations in Somalia to UNOSOM II in May 1993.

Most U.S. forces were redeployed from Somalia, leaving approximately 4,000 U.S. troops, including 1,200 members of an elite Quick Reaction Force stationed on U.S. Navy ships offshore and under independent U.S. command.[19] After UNITAF withdrawal, Somalia's security situation quickly deteriorated as the UNOSOM II military

---

[17] Brune, 19.
[18] U.S. Army, *United States Forces, Somalia After Action Report*, 232.
[19] Brune, *The United States and Post-Cold War Interventions*, 28.

force was much less capable than the previous U.S.-led UNITAF. Brune summarized

UNOSOM II's significant challenges:

> Following UNITAF's withdrawal on May 4, UNOSOM II officials faced
> two major difficulties: first, they lacked specific plans to change
> Somalia's transitional government into a permanent regime; second
> UNOSOM II's much less powerful military capability made it difficult to
> coerce the Somalian warlords to accept peace. Consequently, within a
> month after UNITAF's withdrawal, UNOSOM II's peacemaking mission
> became a warlord hunting venture.[20]

On June 5, 1993, Pakistani forces were ambushed by Aideed's militia while

conducting a short-notice inspection of a weapons storage site in Mogadishu. Aideed's

forces killed 24 and wounded 57 Pakistani soldiers and wounded one Italian and three

American soldiers.[21] At the urgent request of UNOSOM II, the U.S. Quick Reaction

Force conducted a successful rescue of the remaining Pakistani forces. The United

Nations strongly condemned Aideed and on the following day passed Resolution 837

authorizing UNOSOM II to "take all necessary measures against all those responsible for

the armed attack of 5 June 1993."[22] Resolution 837 led UNOSOM II to adopt an even

more offensive posture and its mission transitioned from a neutral role of peace

enforcement to taking sides and fighting a counter-insurgency campaign.[23] The United

States strongly supported Resolution 837 and per Ambassador Oakley, "Washington was

committed to a world-wide, assertive U.N. peacekeeping role and to nation-building and

---

[20] Brune, 28.

[21] Roger N. Sangvic, *Battle of Mogadishu: Anatomy of a Failure* (Ft Leavenworth, KS: School of Advanced Military Studies, 1999), 7.

[22] U.S. Air Force, Office of Lessons Learned, AF/A9L, *U.S. Air Force Airlift Case Studies-Lessons Learned in Humanitarian Assistance Operations 1990-2005,* by Gary Gault (U.S. Air Force, Washington DC, 2008), 72.

[23] Sangvic, 7.

fostering democracy as a part of U.S. national policy."[24] Resolution 837, in essence, had

committed the United States to fighting a counter-insurgency.[25]

During UNOSOM II operations under Resolution 837, several U.S. troops had

been killed by Aideed's militia. UNOSOM II was fully engaged attempting to capture

Aideed but lacked sufficient resources to accomplish the task as well as focus on any

meaningful political reconciliation in Somalia. In late August, the U.S. Secretary of

Defense directed the deployment of Task Force Ranger to Somalia in response to the

increasing casualties inflicted by Aideed's militia targeting U.S. troops.[26]

In early September 1993, Task Force Ranger conducted several operations against

Aideed's militia and captured a few key clan leaders. However, on September 25th

Somali clans shot down a U.S. helicopter, killing three U.S. crewmembers. With

violence continuing to escalate in Mogadishu, Task Force Ranger conducted a daytime

raid on October 3rd and captured six of Aideed's lieutenants and several militia members.

During the raid, Aideed's militia shot down two U.S. helicopters. The helicopter

catastrophes and ensuing firefight killed 18 and wounded 78 U.S. soldiers[27] and the

Somalis had sustained an estimated 312 deaths and 814 wounded.[28]

Ambassador Oakley later stated that "this incident caused such a negative public

and political reaction across the United States that the Clinton administration was forced

to withdrawal U.S. forces."[29] President Clinton temporarily reinforced U.S. troops in

Somalia immediately after the incident, but Congress indicated that it would terminate

funding for continuance of the operation beyond March of 1994. As a result, U.S. forces

---

[24] Oakley, Tucker and Tilford, 15.
[25] Sangvic, 8.
[26] Ibid., 12.
[27] Oakley, Tucker and Tilford, 16.
[28] Brune, *The United States and Post-Cold War Interventions*, 32.
[29] Oakley, Tucker and Tilford, 16.

were withdrawn from Somalia on March 23, 1994. UNOSOM II departed in March 1995 after the United Nations failed to achieve a political resolution and peace in Somalia.

Conclusions and Lessons Learned

Analysis of U.S. involvement in Somalia from 1992-1994 offers lessons learned that can provide U.S. national leaders and policymakers useful insights to consider in light of using the U.S. military to support future foreign humanitarian assistance operations. The United States used military force to support humanitarian assistance operations in Somalia in an attempt to resolve widespread starvation and famine. However, the intervention, initiated by U.S. leaders with an idealist approach, was not connected to nor supported by clearly identified U.S. national security interests. In Somalia, U.S. interests rested solely on U.S. national leaders' moral imperative to act and their perceived duty to assist as the world's sole superpower. Using Nuechterlein's level of intensity criteria for categorizing national interests, as previously discussed in this study, U.S. national interests in Somalia could be identified as peripheral, meaning the interests "do not seriously affect the well-being of the United States…as a whole is not particularly affected by any given outcome or the impact is negligible."[30]

After UNITAF's initial success during Operation Restore Hope of reducing famine and starvation in Somalia, the U.S.'s involvement in foreign humanitarian assistance operations transformed politically and operationally, through the United Nations, into a robust military peace enforcement and nation-building mission. Somalia was a failed nation state where sectarian and ethnic warfare was the root cause of the humanitarian crisis. The United Nations, supported by the United States, propelled

---

[30] Donald Nuechterlein, *America Recommitted: A Superpower Assesses Its Role in a Turbulent World – Second Edition* (Lexington, KY: University of Lexington Press, 2001), 17-20.

emerging goals of ensuring political stability and subsequent peace to Somalia. The U.S. military was caught in the middle of the escalating political goals, experiencing mission creep in a nation where the United States found it difficult to realize concrete national security interests. The Somalia experience resulted in the Clinton Administration crafting Presidential Decision Directive 25 (PDD-25), U.S. Policy on Reforming Multilateral Peace Operations. The Presidential policy represented a national framework for decision-making on issues of military peacekeeping and peace enforcement operations in light of the post-Cold War period."[31] PDD-25, in essence, prescribed the conditions when U.S. forces would be used and under what conditions in relation to overseas peace operations.

Analysis of U.S. involvement in Somalia illustrates the absence of the dual character of U.S. military engagement overseas that was previously discussed and is a common thread in this study. U.S. leaders used the military in Somalia to pursue idealistic interests that were based on their perceived moral imperative to act. However, the U.S. military involvement in Somalia lacked support for *Realpolitik* interests in terms of supporting clearly identified national security interests. The United States maintained a high moral ground posture during operations in Somalia, but when U.S. casualties mounted, the public and political will for sustaining the foreign humanitarian assistance operations withered away.

U.S. military involvement in Somalia further indicates that the moral and idealist attractiveness of foreign humanitarian assistance operations can lead to an exaggeration of its effectiveness, and helps illustrate why future foreign humanitarian assistance operations should be designed to meet strategic parameters that support U.S. national

---

[31] U.S. President, Presidential Decision Directive/NSC-25 (PDD-25), "U.S. Policy on Reforming Multilateral Peace Operations," *Federal Register*, May 3, 1994.

security interests. The next chapter of this study will identify parameters and provide

recommendations that may be useful for U.S. leaders and policymakers to consider while

making decisions regarding U.S. military involvement in foreign humanitarian assistance

operations.

CHAPTER 5

PARAMETERS AND RECOMMENDATIONS

Making judgments about using the U.S. military to support foreign humanitarian assistance operations will never be easy for U.S. leaders and policymakers. The following discussion will define parameters and provide recommendations for U.S. leaders and policymakers to consider when linking U.S. military involvement in foreign humanitarian assistance operations to U.S. national security interests.

U.S. leaders will likely continue to face difficult decisions when determining whether or not to use its military to support foreign humanitarian assistance operations. It is important to understand the premise of current U.S. strategic guidance and U.S. leaders' political perspectives as the intellectual foundation for which strategic parameters will be defined. As the study previously identified, the decision to use the U.S. military to support foreign humanitarian assistance operations often lies between Realism and Idealism political theories; analysis of contemporary U.S. strategic guidance and policy supports this premise. From a realist perspective, supporting "survival" and "vital" national interests (using Nuechterlein's definitions) will likely be an easy and palatable decision for U.S. leaders, hence the clarity of the Berlin Airlift. However, some U.S. leaders may also be tempted from an idealist perspective, as were the Bush and Clinton administrations in Somalia, to support "major" or "peripheral" national interests in an effort to promote "respect for universal values at home and around the world."[1]

The parameters for using the U.S. military to support foreign humanitarian assistance can be grouped under two conditions: humanitarian assistance operations

---

[1] U.S. President. *National Security Strategy* (Washington DC: Government Printing Office, May 2010), 17.

conducted in hostile/non-permissive environments and humanitarian assistance operations conducted in non-hostile/permissive environments.[2] As a general premise, the United States should refrain from using the U.S. military to support foreign humanitarian assistance operations in hostile/non-permissive environments unless the operations support survival or vital national security interests. A hostile/non-permissive environment can be characterized by security enforcement requirements in which the U.S. military is tasked to establish and maintain security conditions for the provision of foreign humanitarian assistance. Hostile/non-permissive operations require the use of military forces for protection and armed escorts for convoys, shelters for dislocated civilians, and security of multinational forces.[3] As evidenced by U.S. military involvement in Somalia, the distinction between foreign humanitarian assistance and armed conflict can easily and rapidly blur. Hostile/non-permissive foreign humanitarian assistance operations put the lives of U.S. military personnel at risk and should be avoided unless in direct support of U.S. survival or vital national security interests.

It is difficult to predict a situation where U.S. military involvement in a foreign humanitarian assistance operation would be directly linked to survival or vital national security interests, although it is not beyond the realm of possibilities; U.S. leaders and policymakers cannot completely discount this type of situation. Hypothetically, an extreme natural disaster in Mexico, for example, could propagate massive migration into the United States and impact vital national security interests. National strategic guidance and policy should clearly articulate how U.S. military involvement in foreign

---

[2] The discussion in the following paragraphs draws from Ambassador Robert B. Oakley and David Tucker, edited by Earl Tilford, Jr., *Two Perspectives on Interventions and Humanitarian Operations* (Carlisle Barracks: Army War College, 1997), 28-33.

[3] U.S. Joint Chiefs of Staff, *Foreign Humanitarian Assistance*, Joint Publication 3-29 (Washington DC: Joint Chiefs of Staff, March 17, 2009), x.

humanitarian assistance operations supports national security interests. Guidance and policy should also propose conditions that should be met before the U.S. military is used to intervene in non-permissive/hostile environments.

There should be as little ambiguity as possible in strategic guidance and policy to limit U.S. military involvement in foreign humanitarian assistance operations. U.S. Senate Bill 3176, if passed into law, would authorize the U.S. Congress to deliberate and ultimately make the decision for U.S. military involvement supporting foreign humanitarian assistance operations in non-permissive/hostile environments. Deliberations among U.S. elected leaders required by Senate Bill 3176 would help political leaders, particularly those with an idealist perspective, to analyze more thoroughly the possible effects of using the U.S. military to support foreign humanitarian assistance operations in non-permissive/hostile environments. Deliberations would also help identify the root cause of the humanitarian crisis so U.S. leaders would be less inclined to simply treat the humanitarian symptoms of a conflict, as illustrated by the United States' humanitarian intervention in Somalia and subsequent mission-creep that led to eventual security enforcement operations. A significant challenge posed by Senate Bill 3176, if passed, could be the considerable amount of time required to deliberate the humanitarian assistance or disaster relief response options. This challenge is not unrealistic, especially in light of how Congress and the Senate have performed lately. One would hope the Senate would feel a sense of urgency during deliberations as a timely response to crisis events is of significant importance; the passing of each day more people are susceptible of dying in most humanitarian assistance or disaster relief situations.

U.S. military support for foreign humanitarian assistance operations conducted in non-hostile/permissive environments should also serve a strategic purpose and directly support U.S. national security interests. Although non-hostile/permissive operations do not put the lives of U.S. military personnel at risk, they should be limited as much as possible to avoid overextending and potentially lowering the readiness of U.S. military forces. The United States' initial considerations for assisting in foreign humanitarian crisis should be through USAID, assisted by domestic and international nongovernmental relief agencies. U.S. military involvement in foreign humanitarian assistance operations should be reserved to supporting unique humanitarian assistance requirements that only U.S. military forces can provide in order to alleviate immediate human suffering and save lives. The U.S. military is well-suited for providing rapid, large-scale logistical, medical and other expertise for humanitarian assistance for requirements that often exceed the capabilities of USAID, the host nation, or international nongovernmental relief agencies. Much of the military capability is expeditionary in nature and can be an effective stop-gap measure until civilian capacity can assume the humanitarian assistance operations. Understanding that time is of the essence in disaster relief and foreign humanitarian assistance operations, the United States should leverage the U.S. military's unique capabilities, but U.S. military involvement should be limited in scope and duration. Political objectives and clearly defined mission termination criteria should be identified before commencement of any military operation in support of foreign humanitarian assistance.

CONCLUSION

U.S. military involvement in foreign humanitarian assistance operations demonstrates U.S. goodwill and support for national governments in times of need, and offers the United States an opportunity to demonstrate U.S. values abroad, support human rights, and enhance regional security. Assessing the operational environment of the world today, one can reasonably assume that military support for foreign humanitarian assistance requirements will continue to outpace capabilities and resources. Absent clearly defined parameters for engaging in foreign humanitarian assistance operations, the United States will risk squandering military and economic resources, divert high demand and low density assets, and lower overall readiness of U.S. military forces—all while pursuing limited objectives in places of marginal national security interests. To maintain a proper balance U.S. military involvement in foreign humanitarian assistance operations should meet strategic parameters that support U.S. national security interests.

This study began with a review of select terms to interpret and establish respective definitions and clarify the vernacular used in the context of foreign humanitarian assistance operations. Doctrinal definitions were analyzed and largely determined inadequate in terms of standardization across the whole of government. The non-standardized definitions can lead to U.S. government interagency confusion which often contributes to leaders, policymakers and agencies talking past one another. Further, the study examined Realism and Idealism international relations theories to develop an understanding of the foundation of U.S. national security strategy and the approach U.S.

leaders may use to determine how and when to use the military to intervene in foreign humanitarian assistance operations.

A review and analysis of U.S. strategic guidance and policy informed and developed an understanding of contemporary strategic perspectives provided by U.S. national leaders and policymakers. U.S. national interest and levels of national interests were analyzed in the context of how the United States should use its military to support national security interests through foreign humanitarian assistance operations. Parameters were described suggesting the United States should refrain from using the U.S. military to support foreign humanitarian assistance operations in hostile/non-permissive environments unless the operations support survival or vital national security interests.

The case study of the Berlin Airlift provided positive illustration of using a realist political approach to achieve U.S. national security interests using military soft power in support of foreign humanitarian assistance operations. Conversely, analysis of idealist U.S. military intervention in Somalia, hampered by political challenges, provided negative illustration where military activities in support of foreign humanitarian assistance operations did not fully support U.S. national security interests.

In summary, analysis of contemporary U.S. strategic guidance and historical case studies indicates that U.S. leaders and policymakers may be prone to succumb to the attractiveness and effectiveness of foreign humanitarian assistance operations, particularly with regard to the operation's potential to promote and advance U.S. national security interests. Moreover, as learned in Somalia, U.S. leaders and policymakers can often fail to assess appropriate risk and determine plausible termination criteria for foreign humanitarian assistance operations.

In light of almost certain budget cuts of the next decade, it will be critical that U.S. leaders not overextend the U.S. military, waste scarce national resources, and lower the readiness of military forces by committing the U.S. military to operations that are not connected to larger national security interests. U.S. leaders and policymakers must have the wherewithal to acknowledge that the United States cannot afford to use the U.S. military intervene in every foreign humanitarian crisis without accepting undue risk to the readiness of military forces. The parameters outlined in this study may serve useful in guiding U.S. leaders and policymakers.

BIBLIOGRAPHY

Allard, Kenneth. *Somalia Operations: Lessons Learned.* Washington DC: Institute for National Strategic Studies, National Defense University, 1995.

Art, Robert J. *A Grand Strategy for America.* Ithaca, NY: Cornell University Press, 2003.

"The Berlin Airlift." *Mobility Forum*, No. 3 (May/Jun 1998, 1998): 14-5, http://search.proquest.com/docview/213803329?accountid=12686.

Brune, Lester H. *The United States and Post-Cold War Interventions: Bush and Clinton in Somalia, Haiti, and Bosnia, 1992-1998.* Claremont, CA: Regina Books, 1998.

Bush, George H.W., President, "Humanitarian Crisis in Somalia," *U.S. Department of State Dispatch* (December 14, 1992): 877.

Chairman of the Joint Chiefs of Staff. *The National Military Strategy of the United States of America.* Washington DC: Department of Defense, February, 2011.

————. *2010 Joint Professional Military Education (JPME) Special Areas of Emphasis (SAEs),* May 17, 2010. Washington DC: Department of Defense, 17 May 2010.

Chossudovsky, Michel. "The Militarization of Emergency Aid to Haiti: Is it a Humanitarian Operation or an Invasion?" *Global Research.* January 15, 2010. http://www.globalresearch.ca (accessed September 9, 2012).

Clair, Carol D. *Humanitarian Assistance and the Elements of Operational Design.* Fort Leavenworth: School of Advanced Military Studies, 1993.

Clay, Lucius D. *Decision in Germany.* New York: Double Day & Co., 1950.

Congressional Research Service, Report R41250. *Quadrennial Defense Review 2010: Overview and Implications for National Security Planning,* by Stehpen Daggett, May 17, 2010. Washington, DC: Government Printing Office, 2010.

Cuny, Frederick C. "Use of the Military in Humanitarian Relief," speech given at Niinsalo, Finland Military Academy, November, 1989. Frontline, PBS Online. http://www.pbs.org/wgbh/pages/frontline/shows/cuny/laptop/humanrelief.html (accessed September 9, 2012).

Department of Defense Security Cooperation Agency. *Fiscal Year 2012 Budget Estimates Overseas Humanitarian, Disaster Assistance, and Civic Aid.* Defense Security Cooperation Agency. Washington, DC: Government Printing Office, 2011.

Donovan, Robert. *Conflict and Crisis: The Presidency of Harry S. Truman, 1945-1948.* New York: W.W. Norton and Company, Inc, 1977.

Dunn, Edward, and Richard Anderson, Clark Hanson, William Paulin, Stuart O'Black. *U.S. Army Role in Humanitarian Operations and National Interest.* Fort Bliss: United States Army Sergeants Major Academy, 2007.

Eberhart, Paul B. *Grand Strategy of the United States: A Study of the Process.* Norfolk: Joint Forces Staff College, 2009.

Estep, David G. *Air Mobility: The Strategic Use of Nonlethal Airpower.* Maxwell Air Force Base, School of Advanced Airpower Studies, 1994.

Fixdal, Mona and Dan Smith. "Humanitarian Intervention and Just War." *Mershon International Studies Review* 42, no. 2 (November 1998): 283-312.

Gates, Robert M. "Helping Others Defend Themselves: The Future of U.S. Security Assistance." *Foreign Affairs* (May-June 2010): 2-6.

Harrington, Daniel F. *Berlin on the Brink: The Blockade, the Airlift, and the Early Cold War.* Lexington, Ky.: University Press of Kentucky, 2012.

Hinson, David R. *U.S. Military Interaction with Humanitarian Assistance Organizations During Small-Scale Contingencies.* Maxwell Air Force Base: Air University, 1998.

Joint Center for Operational Analysis. *International Humanitarian Assistance and Disaster Relief Operations.* Power-point presentation, U.S. Joint Forces Command. Suffolk, 16 January 2007.

———. *USSOUTHCOM and JTF-Haiti...Some Challenges and Considerations in Forming a Joint Task Force.* Open-file report, U.S. Joint Forces Command. Suffolk, 24 June 2010.

Joint and Coalition Operational Analysis (JCOA). *Decade of War, Volume 1, Enduring Lessons from the Past Decade of Operations (June 2012).* Open-file report, U.S. Joint Chiefs of Staff. Suffolk, 2012.

Labbe, Jeremie. *Rethinking Humanitarianism: Adapting to 21st Century Challenges.* New York: International Peace Institute, November, 2012.

Mason, Elmer R. *Leveraging Humanitarian Assistance (HA) in Support of the National Security Strategy.* Carlisle Barracks: Army War College, 2011.

Miyamoto, Saiko. *Strategic Communication in Pursuit of National Interests.* Carlisle Barracks: Army War College, 2012.

Morris, Eric. *Blockade; Berlin and the Cold War*. New York: Stein and Day, 1973.

Nye, Joseph S., Jr. *Soft Power, The Means to Success in World Politics*. New York: PublicAffairs, 2004.

Nuechterlein, Donald E. *America Recommitted: A Superpower Assesses Its Role in a Turbulent World – Second Edition*. Lexington, KY: University of Kentucky Press, 2001.

Nuechterlein, Donald E. *Defiant Superpower: The New American Hegemony*. Washington DC: Potomac Books Inc, 2005.

Oakley, Robert B., U.S. Ambassador, and David Tucker, edited by Earl Tilford, Jr. *Two Perspectives on Interventions and Humanitarian Operations*. Carlisle Barracks: Army War College, 1997.

Poole, Walter S. *The Effort to Save Somalia, August 1992 - March 1994*. Washington DC: Joint History Office, Office of the Joint Chiefs of Staff, 2005.

Sangvic, Roger N. *Battle of Mogadishu: Anatomy of a Failure*. Fort Leavenworth, KS: School of Advanced Studies, U.S. Army Command and General Staff College, 1998.

Sebastiaan J.H. Rietjens, Hans Voordijk, and Sirp J. De Boer. "Coordinating Humanitarian Operations in Peace Support Missions." *Disaster Prevention and Management* 16, no. 1 (2007): 56-69, http://search.proquest.com/docview/214384470?accountid=12686.

Sharp, T. W., R. Yip, and J. D. Malone. "US Military Forces and Emergency International Humanitarian Assistance." *JAMA: The Journal of the American Medical Association* 272, no. 5 (1994): 386-90.

Tine, Gregory C. "Berlin Airlift: Logistics, Humanitarian Aid, and Strategic Success." *Army Logistician* 37, no. 5 (Sep/Oct 2005, 2005): 39-41.

Tunner, William H. *The Berlin Airlift*. Ramstein Air Base, Germany: Office of History, United States Air Forces in Europe, 1998. Booklet is a reprint of the chapter entitled "Berlin Airlift" from *Over the Hump*, Lieutenant General William H. Tunner's autobiography.

Tunner, William H. *Over the Hump*. New York: Duell, Sloan and Pearce, 1964.

U.S. Air Force. Office of Air Force Lessons Learned, AF/A9L. *U.S. Air Force Airlift Case Studies-Lessons Learned in Humanitarian Assistance Operations, 1990-2005*, by Gary Gault. U.S. Air Force, Washington DC, 2008.

U.S. Army. *United States Forces, Somalia After Action Report and Historical Overview*:
   The United States Army in Somalia, 1992-1994. Center of Military History.
   Washington DC, 2003.

U.S. Congress. Senate. *Military Humanitarian Operations Act of 2012.* S3176. 112th
   Cong., 2d sess. (May 14, 2012).

U.S. Department of Defense. *DoD Directive 5100.46: Foreign Disaster Relief (FDR).*
   Washington DC: Department of Defense, 6 July 2012.

———. Historical Office. *History of the Office of the Secretary of Defense: The
   Formative Years 1947-1950,* by Steven L. Rearden. Department of Defense.
   Washington DC, 1984.

———. *National Defense Strategy.* Washington DC: Secretary of Defense, June 2008.

———. *Quadrennial Defense Review Report.* Washington DC: Secretary of Defense,
   February, 2010.

———. *Sustaining U.S. Global Leadership: Priorities for the 21st Century Defense.*
   Washington DC: Secretary of Defense, January, 2012.

———. *The United States Army in Somalia, 1992-1994.* Pub 70-81-1. Washington DC:
   Chief of Military History, no date.

U.S. Department of State and U.S. Agency for International Development. *Strategic
   Plan: Fiscal Years 2007-2012.* Washington DC: Department of State, May 7, 2007.

U.S. Department of State. *Standardized Program Structure and Definitions*, April 8,
   2010. http://www.state.gov/f/c24132.htm (accessed November 20, 2012).

———. *Quadrennial Diplomacy and Development Review.* Washington DC:
   Department of State, 2010.

U.S. Joint Chiefs of Staff. *Capstone Concept for Joint Operations.* Washington DC: Joint
   Chiefs of Staff, September 10, 2012.

———. *Civil-Military Operations, Joint Publication 3-57.* Washington DC: Joint Chiefs
   of Staff, July 8, 2008.

———. *Department of Defense Dictionary of Military and Associated Terms, Joint
   Publication 1-02.* Washington DC: Joint Chiefs of Staff, April 12, 2001.

———. *Doctrine for the Armed Forces of the United States, Joint Publication 1.*
   Washington DC: Joint Chiefs of Staff, March 20, 2009.

———. *Foreign Humanitarian Assistance, Joint Publication 3-29*. Washington DC: Joint Chiefs of Staff, March 17, 2009.

———. *Interagency, Intergovernmental Organization, and Nongovernmental Organization Coordination during Joint Operations, Vol I, Joint Publication 3-08*. Washington DC: Joint Chiefs of Staff, March 17, 2006.

———. *Civil-Military Operations, Joint Publication 3-57*. Washington DC: Joint Chiefs of Staff, July 8, 2008.

———. *Multinational Operations, Joint Publication 3-16*. Washington DC: Joint Chiefs of Staff, March 7, 2007.

U.S. President. Executive Order 12966. "Foreign Disaster Assistance." *Federal Register* (July 18, 1995).

———. *National Security Strategy*. Washington DC: Government Printing Office, May 2010.

———. Presidential Decision Directive/NSC-25 (PDD-25). "U.S. Policy on Reforming Multilateral Peace Operations." *Federal Register* (May 3, 1994).

Waghelstein, John D. *Military-To-Military Contacts: Personal Observations—The El Salvador Case*. U.S. Military Group, El Salvador Country Team. Fall, 2002.

Walt, Stephen M. "International Relations: One World, Many Theories." *Foreign Policy*. 110 (1998): 29-35.

Wheeler, Victoria and Adele Harmer. *Resetting the Rules of Engagement, Trends and Issues in Military-Humanitarian Relations*. London, United Kingdom: Overseas Development Institute, March, 2006.

Yarger, Harry. *Strategy and the National Security Professional: Strategic Thinking and Strategy Formulation in the 21st Century*. Westport: Praeger Security International, 2008.